Building a
Great
Marriage!

Books by Paul J. Bucknell

Allowing the Bible to speak to our lives today!

+ Overcoming Anxiety: Finding Peace, Discovering God
+ Reaching Beyond Mediocrity: Being an Overcomer
+ The Life Core: Discovering the Heart of Great Training
+ The Godly Man: When God Touches a Man's Life
+ Redemption Through the Scriptures
+ Godly Beginnings for the Family
+ Principles and Practices of Biblical Parenting
+ Building a Great Marriage
+ Christian Premarital Counseling Manual for Counselors
+ Relational Discipleship: Cross Training
+ Running the Race: Overcoming Lusts
+ Genesis: The Book of Foundations
+ Book of Romans: The Living Commentary
+ Book of Romans: Bible Study Questions
+ Bible Study Questions for the Book of Ephesians
+ Walking with Jesus: Abiding in Christ
+ Inductive Bible Studies in Titus
+ 1 Peter Bible Study Questions: Living in a Fallen World.
+ Take Your Next Step into Ministry
+ Training Leaders for Ministry
+ Study Guide for Jonah: Understanding God's Heart

Check out these valuable resources at
www.foundationsforfreedom.net

Building A Great Marriage!

Finding Faith, Forgiveness and Friendship

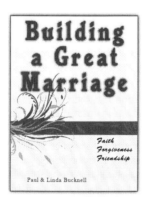

Paul and Linda Bucknell

Building a Great Marriage! Finding Faith, Forgiveness and Friendship

by Paul and Linda Bucknell

Copyright © 2002, 2009, 2013 by Paul J. Bucknell

Paperback:

ISBN-10: 1619930277

ISBN-13: 978-1-61993-027-8

Also in e-Book:

ISBN-10: 1619930161

ISBN-13: 978-1-61993-016-2

Published by Paul J. Bucknell. All profits go to Biblical Foundations for Freedom, a nonprofit organization releasing God's truth to the world!

www.foundationsforfreedom.net

3276 Bainton St.
Pittsburgh, Pennsylvania,15212 USA

info@foundationsforfreedom.net

Dedication

In Dedication to the Beauty of the Lord God

Beauty and perfection are in Him only found,

Our Lord, Our Maker, Our Designer.

In marriage He created a picture

That provides a glimpse into love's greatest heights.

We encounter and respond to Christ's unwavering love,

And our marriages become a display

Of His magnanimous love in this cold world below.

Table of Contents

Section #3: Friendship

Preface

Do you remember those grand hopes you had for your marriage? Don't throw them away too quickly. God uses these hopes to inspire us to have great marriages!

Although couples start off their marriages with high ideals, many of these quickly give up their dreams of having a great marriage and resign themselves to maintaining a less than desirable marriage, discolored by hard words and thoughts. Even within weeks or days of a glorious ceremony, they can become willing to trade their precious dreams for broken spirits. The promises, hopes and glitters of joy are all replaced with what feels like a lifetime of mistrust and selfishness. They pull back their open trust and get ready for the long siege.

It is time that we recapture our dreams and again seek God to give us those great marriages. Our Lord has given us these grand hopes because this is what He really wants for our lives. The dreams are good and are meant to give us a taste of what God wants for our lives. After all, He designed marriage and knows what is best for us. The problem is not that these goals are beyond our reach, but that we expect them to come so easily, as if it was a gift rather than something to work toward. Great marriages need to be built. They do not come about by accident.

If our marriages are carefully built according to the design of our Maker, then strong foundations will enable us to build elegant and glorious unions. This book is filled with practical suggestions on how to build a great marriage, whether you are getting along okay or facing serious marital difficulties. Study questions are available at the end of each chapter.

Building a Great Marriage focuses on three important building blocks for a great marriage: faith, forgiveness and friendship. Faith, chapters 1-4, enables us to gain God's view of marriage. This is where we learn His design for marriage and how it operates. Forgiveness, chapters 5-7, gently shows us how to restore broken marriages and relationships so that a couple can then build upon God's design. Friendship, chapters 8-10, describes the pathway for a beautiful intimate marriage.

As we step back and begin to understand the mysterious and powerful principles at work within marriage, our hopes will leap forward, God's ways will be desired in our hearts and relationships, and we will seek Him in this area. We all can have great marriages as we lean upon God's grace and depend on His Word.

The principles of marriage are not hard to understand. They are in fact incredibly simple. But like a beautiful snowflake, they are intricate in design and so easily destroyed. If we are ever going to see and apply these incredible principles to our marriages, then we need to step away from the voices of the world and listen closely to what God says about marriage. He will guide us step by step into the fullness of His promises, even if we are presently far from obtaining that dream.

Many marriage books and conferences encourage you to remove yourselves from the real world to improve your marriage. I flatly disagree. If a marriage is going to grow and thrive, it must do so in real life situations – limited budgets, being tired, unable to get away, etc. With eight children, four of them presently being home-schooled, we have not have been able to have many of those romantic vacations! God's principles, however, powerfully work even in our typical and difficult marriage situations.

God has seeded high hopes into our hearts so that marriages will grow, thrive and reflect His glorious ways. Should we not turn to Him and His Word to obtain rich, intimate and beautiful marriages, all built on His intricate design? Let's now learn together how to build those great marriages. Each chapter has study questions to facilitate a deeper understanding and application of key principles, for the individual couple or a small group.

Paul J. Bucknell

August, 2012

Happily married for more than thirty-five years!

Founder and President of Biblical Foundations for Freedom

Section #1: Faith

Chapters #1-4

Gaining God's View of Marriage

Building a
Great Marriage

#1 Restoring Hope To Your Marriage

How would you answer the question, "What makes a great marriage?" Many people have difficulty describing the elements of a wonderful marriage. Most of these couples have not even seen a great marriage in operation. No wonder great marriages are so rare. Where have all the models gone? We have not seen them. We cannot even define what a great marriage is like!

Lost hope

If we took a survey, we would discover that not a few couples to some degree have given up hope on their marriage. We are not only speaking of the divorced or separated, but of those that are still together. If they would be honest they would rate their marriage from bad to horrible (men typically are far more positive than their wives). Perhaps you are one of those spouses who have given up hope that things can get better. You are not alone.

Marriage intensifies problems rather than solves them.

There are signs that tell the story of your lost hope. Heart signs for poor marriages include taking one's marriage for granted and general discontent. Disrespect and bitterness have taken the place of excitement and delight for one's partner. More tragic signs of betrayal include pornography and sexual affairs (whether in thought or in reality). When one is not content at home, he or she goes elsewhere to be distracted and often finds another person that promises more than one's present spouse.

Things were different before

But things were different before, weren't they? Despite signs that things were not perfect between you and your fiancé, in the beginning you were willing to overlook the imperfections. You were willing to commit your life and all that you had to one another. This is because you had hope. You believed those problems were next to nothing in comparison to being married to that special person. Perhaps being a bit naïve, you thought the problems would solve themselves by having that one marry you! Those who have been married now see that marriage intensifies rather than solves problems! But is giving up hope the solution? Certainly not!

Restoration of hope is the theme of this chapter. Hope does not solve problems, but it does put us on the right track so we can work out the many large and small difficulties that we face in our marriages. Without hope, you and I will avoid the problems until catastrophic decisions further erode the marriage relationship.

Some have suggested that it is good for spouses to argue (I can't imagine Jesus communicating with His disciples in this way). They mean, I think, that at least these couples still have some hope left for their marriage. They are still communicating. Otherwise, they would not argue or fight at all. This might be true in a limited sense, but it is not helpful to make arguments a sign of life. They certainly are not the end goal for our marriages.

We prefer to focus on reconciliation that leads to peace and hope. Many couples do not know how to peaceably resolve differences or thrive in intimate conversation. They have no clue how to work through differences and misunderstandings. The spouses only know how to preserve their privileges and rights via arguments and fights. Hope will, however, help you become the kind of spouse who will learn how to work with God in your marriage.

God's view of marriage

Marriage is not, as most people believe, a mere human agreement with legal ramifications. This is the secular view of marriage. God's Word, however, gives us an accurate perspective. God Himself instituted marriage. God declared the two to be one in Genesis 2:24. Every marriage is divine in nature because of God's creative Word.

> *"For this cause a man shall leave his father and his mother,*
> *and shall cleave to his wife; and they shall become one flesh."*

This is seen even more clearly by the way Jesus spoke of marriage in Mark 10:9, "What therefore God has joined together, let no man separate." Every marriage has been joined together by God. No one should treat marriage as a mere man-made union, even among unbelievers.

Male ⚬═══⚬ Female
Marriage Contract

This is not God's concept of marriage.

Whether a marriage is performed in court or in church, a man and woman take oaths before their mighty Creator. In every marriage, then, there are three components: God, husband, and wife. Therefore, when one spouse gets serious about God's part in the marriage, great hopes

unfold.[1] One now has a majority! God greatly desires to pour forth His work of grace in every marriage. The Lord is looking for spouses who will seriously apply His Word.

The divine marriage institution means that both Christians and unbelievers are all accountable to God for the way they treat their spouses and generally

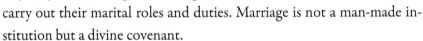

carry out their marital roles and duties. Marriage is not a man-made institution but a divine covenant.

How do we revive hope? In this chapter we want to tackle the problem of hopelessness head on. Good changes do not happen until faith and hope are restored.[2] Only then will one begin to reach the point where one's marriage can grow.

---

[1] Hope for a great marriage is not deluded belief. Hope aligns itself with the promises, principles and purposes of God's Word. For example, should a wife who left her husband for another man be hopeful for her new marriage? Any hope for that new marriage would have to be rooted in sincere repentance from being an adulteress. Unless conviction bears its fruit of repentance, then hope of a good marriage is a delusion that leads down the broad road leading to destruction.

[2] This principle is true whether it be for our marriage or any aspect of the Christian life.

Observations of Marriage

Let's first identify some basic observations about marriage.

- ❖ Good marriages follow God's design.

- ❖ Bad marriages do not follow God's design.

- ❖ Mediocre marriages have not fully embraced God's design.

Notice that our standard for harmony is based on God's design – not a person's feelings. Since God designed marriage, the closer we adopt that original plan, the better the marriage. This is true in a positive way as well as a negative one. If a marriage is doing well, then the couple is to some degree doing some right things. If a couple does not have a happy marriage, then they should recognize that they have somehow departed from God's design.

This understanding enables us to find a right approach. If a couple has a poor marriage, then it is easy for them to accuse each other and perhaps blame God. This places them right where the evil one wants them – without hope. But if that same couple can accept that they have fallen from God's design (even if they do not know how), then they can turn to God with hope for improvement. They only need to discover God's principles and by His grace carry them out.

Here are four observations about how God works in our lives and marriages. They are important to remember both for your marriage and for others. If we do not accept these biblical perspectives on how God interacts with His people, then we will give up hope before we see any real improvement.

- ✦ God wants to build great marriages.

+ God has a way to restore a broken marriage.

+ God works with those who are listening to Him.

+ God leads us back by living by His design.

These truths are always true for God's people. Some of our readers might not yet know God. It is important to get to know God through Jesus Christ so that God will especially help and care for us. Once we are a follower of Jesus, we not only find forgiveness for our disobedient way but become God's child.

For example, if a wife learns how God forgives her of all of her rebellious and stubborn ways through believing that Jesus died on the cross for her, then she can find God's help to pass this kind grace on to her unkind husband. For purposes of this book, we assume the readers have found God's grace in Christ.

Always turn to Hope

Always turn to hope. This is the first step to renewing marriages. You, like others, will no doubt face thoughts about giving up on your marriage. You might believe that you cannot make those needed changes or that your spouse will never reform.

Once we give up hope on being able to improve some aspect of our marriage, we tolerate less than desirable conditions. We see this occur when a man thinks about trying to give up pornography. He will hear, "You can't do it." "You tried it before." "It won't make a difference." All of these statements support the main conclusion that the evil one wants you to make – give up!

A wife might have overcooked dinner in the oven again. Her husband thought he was patient, but this is the third time. He is very irritated, inconsiderate and blurts out some rude remarks. She is thinking of rudely responding. "I'll serve him what he deserves – a burnt supper." "He didn't even ask about my day when he came home!" "I'll just go out with my 'real' friends. Maybe he will learn to appreciate me."

Two Signs

There are two signs of giving up. The inward signs are not as evident as the outward signs but both are detectable if one is looking for them. For example, the lack of contentment with one's spouse often results in the outward sign of a very busy life. Why spend time with each other if he or she does not find what he is looking for at home. Along with this comes the discovery that there is little attraction to be together. This can be seen by the way one is attracted more to others, even if it is in just a romantic novel or a television series.

SIGNS OF GIVING UP	
Inward Signs	*Outward Signs*
Lack of contentment	Distracted by busy lives
"Cold shoulder"	Critical attitude
Bitterness or spirit of revenge	Pornography and seductive movies
Unforgiving spirit	Easily angered
Disrespectful attitude	Disrespectful words about spouse

Bitterness of the heart (inward sign) finds little room for sexual pleasures so one or both spouses engage in pornography, seductive movies, or affairs. An unforgiving spirit (inward) can be seen by how easily a spouse gets angry over little things. Although disrespect for one's spouse is an inward sign, it can be noticed by impolite words.

Again, we see how cleverly these tempting thoughts are threaded together. They direct us to give up hope and respond in sin.[3] The Lord, however, always wants us to turn in the direction of hope. It is here that we will find strength to do His will.

Personal Application: A Marriage Building Project

Let's get more practical. Think of your spouse right now. (If you are not married, you might think of your past spouse or the relationship between your parents.) You probably have given up hope on each other in one or more areas. This is the assignment.

+ Write down three or four areas in which you have given up hope in your marriage relationship. Keep reading for further clarification and examples.

+ You can add to this list other areas that you still have hope in and are working on.

This will be called our "hope list" because these are the very areas in which we need hope.
Write them as positively as possible. These hopes often hide behind our assumptions and expectations about life. In order to complete this assignment, we will need to keep several questions in mind.

---

[3] There are many words and phrases that convey a spirit of giving up. It is important that you begin to detect what these phrases are so that you can quickly spot and reject them. Write these phrases down and then you will see how the evil one has been toying with your life and marriage through these thoughts. Replace them with God's thoughts (thoughts from scriptures, that which is true and good (see Philippians 4:8-9).

(1) How do you identify these areas of lost hope?

These are the areas in which you once had hope. If you were recently married, you will be more aware of some grand expectations before your wedding. But now through some startling situations, your hopes have disappeared. You have given up hope. Write these hopes and expectations down.

Others have been married for a while. You can best spot these areas of lost hope by your areas of struggle. What are you frustrated about? What do you argue about? Get down to the real root issues. Like the source of a well, your expectations lie deep down below the surface. Some things will take a while before being detected. Others are right on your lips! Finish the statement, "I wish my wife (or husband) would ...." Write your thoughts down.

Let me give you an illustration. Suppose you wanted your wife just to do what you said, but every time you ask her to do something (or so it seems), she contests you. You don't want to fight with her but more often than not, it seems you end up yelling at her. Bitterness has now settled in. You tend to avoid her. You are beginning to give up hope of any change and you therefore lessen your commitment to the relationship. Write this hope down, "I hope my wife will submit to me with a cheerful spirit." Make sure you write down the hope of what you want to happen rather than implant your anger or disappointment into what is written. For example, "I wish my lousy wife would shape up." This is far too negative.

(2) Isn't it too late?

Some hopes which are written down might seem impossible to achieve. The issues have gone beyond management. The focus has shifted from preserving sanity to damage control – not to let things become utterly reckless. Let's look at an example.

Say you were always hoping that you would be able to talk deeply about the issues of life with your husband, but he has never seemed interested and has always busied himself in his own activities. Now you have become silently bitter as he watches television or spends time with his friends instead of wanting to spend time with you. Although you still live together as a married couple, you almost live two completely separate lives, each not trusting the other.

This situation is not too late. Is the couple still married and both alive? God wants every couple to turn to Him for help. It does not matter how much time has passed – even twenty years. You can still have hope because you believe God is part of your marriage. God is the God of miracles.

The situation gets increasingly difficult when both spouses are not eager to resolve things. They have no hope and therefore face deep problems. But when we have hope and trust in God's work, then there is much room for improvement. The process of building a great marriage will no doubt take time. But since a couple is married for life, one may as well start working on improving it!

(3) Do we all have areas of hopelessness?

Our loss of hope looks different as we go through different stages of married life. Even good marriages could be better. We need to see whether or not our expectations (or hopes) are correct (we will examine this more in another chapter). Sometimes our expectations are conjured up by a materialistic and pleasure-seeking world. We must reject these ambitions. More often than not, though, we know when our marriage is missing some key element.

Even in good marriages, spouses can lose hope for improvement in one or two problem areas. A husband might be careless about where he drops his dirty laundry. A wife might worry about finances. A husband might be too free spending for his own projects and ignore other more basic needs (or so the wife thinks). Some couples focus their hopes on key areas needing improvement while others on less urgent wishes.

One major problem consists of couples not knowing what makes a great marriage. They have no idea what good things can happen in a marriage. This confusion makes sense. If our parents were not happily married, we do not have a good model for married life. Our search for a great marriage will come step by step. We first need to improve one area of our marriage and then we will be able to face another. Otherwise, we will be easily discouraged. Those couples with good marriages usually are still taking such steps, though the area of improvement is more refined.

(4) Isn't it dangerous to focus on what we don't have?

The wedding is the bud. Marriage is the unfolding of the beautiful flower. Although we are pointing out areas of discontent, it is for a good purpose. We are exposing areas in which God wants to work. By avoiding them, resentment and bitterness arise until a crisis occurs. Through properly prioritizing and dealing with these difficult points, a couple can grow in their unity much like a beautiful pearl develops from a grain of sand irritating an oyster.

Hope reminds us of what ought to be. Hope depends on the power and grace of God for fulfillment. By looking at the problem, we are reacquainted with our inadequacies. By looking to Him for His miraculous grace, we begin to see light in what is very often a dark area of our life. At the same time we expose bad attitudes that have perhaps perpetuated the lack of growth in a certain area. We are not fighting our spouse but working with God to refine our marriage according to His will.

Hope inspires prayer and gets us back on track. Note how God works this out in David's own instructions in Psalm 37:3-5.

"Trust in the LORD, and do good; dwell in the land and cultivate faithfulness.

Delight yourself in the LORD; and He will give you the desires of your heart.
Commit your way to the LORD, trust also in Him, and He will do it."

We take our precious hopes and disappointments and come to God. We focus on our relationship with God and begin to look to Him for solutions. Our trust is in Him. He will begin to bring resolve to some very difficult issues whether they involve lack of communication, incompatibility, or lack of sexual intimacy. "Trust also in Him, and He will do it!"

Truth: Great marriages happen!

As we deal with this issue of hope, we will be confronted head on with a nagging thought, "That is great for him to say, but he obviously does not have my spouse!" I have personally heard "experienced" couples try to pass on a few helpful comments about the facts of real married life to those soon to be married. They mean well. The experienced couple never was able to obtain that beautiful married life and so cautions the young couple about the reality of married life. These comments are sometimes terribly critical and full of hopelessness.

The newlyweds will throw off these "insights" without difficulty and enter marriage. They believe they are different (otherwise they would never plan to marry). Unfortunately, when the couple faces certain disappointments in their new marriage, they often reluctantly accept those fearful "insights" that the experienced couple had previously given them. "Maybe they were right. Marriage is not what we hoped."

Should we feed these new couples despair or hope? Are we being honest when we give them hope? Sure. This does not mean that they will not face problems. They will face problems because each of us has a sinful nature. We need to work with them so that they can learn how to depend upon God's grace and marvelously work through all the difficulties they face. This is why we focus on building a great marriage.

Four Biblical Principles for Marriage

Let's look at four biblical principles that give us hope and confidence for our marriages. There is no better place to go than the Word of God. Here the Designer of marriage reveals His view of marriage in Genesis 2:18-25.

#1 God designed marriage (Genesis 2:18-22)

"Then the LORD God said, "It is not good for the man to be alone; I will make him a helper suitable for him. And out of the ground the LORD God formed every beast of the field and every bird of the sky, and brought them to the man to see what he would call them; and whatever the man called a living creature, that was its name. And the man gave names to all the cattle, and to the birds of the sky, and to every beast of the field, but for Adam there was not found a helper suitable for him. So the LORD God caused a deep sleep to fall upon the man, and he slept; then He took one of his ribs, and closed up the flesh at that place. And the LORD God fashioned into a woman the rib which He had taken from the man, and brought her to the man."

A perfect person. An ideal location. Adam had everything he needed. It was from this beautiful situation that God made and shared a certain observation about the first man Adam, "It is not good for the man to be alone." God had a plan. He was going to make a "helper suitable for him." In order to develop a deeper appreciation for what God would do, God wisely had Adam first become aware of his need by naming all the beasts. Adam became convinced that none of these animals would resolve that deep need he felt. It is at that point where God steps in and does His own special work! He started off with a rib but then fashioned it into the woman. Adam named her Eve.

After forming her, God took time to introduce her to Adam, much like a matchmaker would.[4] God's match, however, was designed almost

---

[4] From this we should gain great hope that God is concerned and involved in the selection of a spouse. It does matter who we marry!

from scratch. She was to be a complement to him rather than a competitor. She was his suitable helper specially designed from Adam's rib. So God made all the necessary factors leading up to marriage. We sometimes think of marriage simply as a binding relationship and forget about the critical elements that make marriage possible. But God didn't! God made both male and female for the purpose of being together in an intimate and long-lasting relationship.

#2 God designed plurality: male and female (Genesis 2:23)

"And the man said, "This is now bone of my bones, and flesh of my flesh; She shall be called Woman, because she was taken out of Man.""

The man was ecstatic. He realized something, which utterly delighted him, was standing beside him. 'Woman' was so named because she was taken from man. Women were designed especially suited to work along their husband's side. There is a similarity between the two genders but with a significant difference despite what modern society is trying to convince us of.

This similarity and difference are both seen in the Hebrew and English words for man and woman. The Hebrew

word for wife adds one letter to the end of the Hebrew word for man (see the chart; remember Hebrew reads from the right). This is also reflected in the English words for man and woman too. Add a 'wo' to man, and we get 'woman.' Or add a 'fe' to male, and we get female.[5]

---

[5] The Hebrew is more accurate and obvious because the words start out the same. The two English words for woman vary at the beginning rather than the end of the word so it is not so noticeable.

#3 God designed oneness (Genesis 2:24)

For this cause a man shall leave his father and his mother, and shall cleave to his wife; and they shall become one flesh.

The plurality of the sexes does not make a marriage. Neither does the sexual act. The term 'one flesh' refers to much more than the sexual relationship between a husband and wife. The phrase 'one flesh' speaks of the relationship as a whole; the sexual union is only one special expression of this.

How do we know this? We can tell there is more to oneness than sexual union by how this oneness is formed and maintained. Oneness is formed by a man leaving the jurisdiction of his parents and forming his own separate entity directly under God accompanied by his lifelong female companion. This special union bears fruit in children as we see in the case of Adam and Eve.

#4 God designed His glory to be revealed in marriage (Genesis 2:25)

And the man and his wife were both naked and were not ashamed.

Mysterious truths are revealed by the marriage relationship. Two people are extraordinarily but surely joined together to make one. The glory of this new entity is the unhindered transparency of the man and woman. They were not ashamed. It is very possible that the original glory was a light that emanated from them as they reflected God's glory.[6]

After rebelling against God, clothes were given to both man and woman. This showed that the openness between the original couple

---

[6] We gather this from several places: (1) Their sense of nakedness upon sin's arrival; (2) Moses' light from his close communion with God; and (3) the expected growing glory as God's people closely commune with God. See www.foundationsforfreedom.net/Topics/Devotions/Devotions012.html for further reflections on this.

could not be easily regained. There were now things in the way. This is not only true physically but emotionally and spiritually. The clothes were a foretaste of Christ which would cover the stain of our separation from and rebellion before God. We will later look carefully at how Paul spoke about the mystery of "oneness."

We should remember that all of this was pronounced and done before the fall of man. Marriage has been and always will be a grand design for human beings on this earth. We can put away our doubts about whether marriage can work out. By God's grace it can and will. A great marriage is not instantaneous. Because of sin, a lot of extra hard work needs to be put into it. Marriage can always be wonderful even in its infant stages, but we need to cultivate it carefully.

Handling Disappointment

Many of us have expectations of the grand things that will occur in our marriages. In most cases, these hopes reflect the good that the Lord wants to establish throughout our married lives. However, we will discover other hopes later on in our marriages. These hopes and expectations become our goals.

When they concur with God's Word, we can be sure they are God's goals for our lives too. The beginning of restoration in our marriages starts when we begin to see what God has planned for our lives. Disappointment over our expectations leads to frustration and doubt. Sometimes we question our spouse's motives and at other times we might even doubt God's purpose. We might think, for example, that God has forgotten us. Indeed He hasn't, but it is easy to fall to this temptation when we do not properly handle disappointment.

By now we should have started working on a list of areas in which we lack hope in our marriages. We have given up hope of improvement in some aspect of our marriage. Our job will be to carefully weigh our ideals in light of God's goals for our marriages. We want to again look to

Him for a great marriage, not just a mediocre one. Let's discuss what we can do with that 'Hope List' in the coming days.

#1 Wait

Don't talk right away about your list of how your marriage could be better. It is not meant to be a list on how bad your spouse has been! To be honest, some of you might never have an opportunity to share this list with your spouse.

#2 Confess

When you have fallen into the temptation of giving up, you need to confess your sin to God. God does not want you to doubt His good plan. Early on you might find other areas of sin in your life that you might confess. Remember that sin discourages us from obtaining God's design.

#3 Ask

Ask the Lord to restore hope to the hopeless areas. It might be something so simple as your husband expressing his gratefulness for your hard work. Or it could be the ability to live with your selfish spouse in love and kindness. It could also have to do with sexual intimacy.

#4 Anticipate

Give God the opportunity to answer your prayer in His time and way. We do this by telling Him and yourself what you want, why you think your marriage should have those things, and a willingness to do what is needed for it to be done, even if it takes a long time. Wives must not nag, hint, or manipulate to get what they wish. Husbands must refuse to commandeer their wives into what they want.

#5 Share

It is natural to want to share your list with your spouse. If your spouse asks to hear your list, then you are free to share it with him or her. If he or she does not ask, then just keep it between you and God. Remember you "two," God and you, are a team working together in hope. Each day you will seek Him for these things and watch how He begins to accomplish this work.

Hope for miracles

God is a God of miracles. Even in the most desperate situations, God can build beautiful and wonderful marriages. Hope is a seed of faith. We are expressing trust in God to work out what is great and wonderful. Hold on to your hope. Think of building your great marriage as a life-long process. We must learn to cherish not only the end goal but also the process of drawing closer to God and our spouse. As you hold onto God and His promises, He surprises us as He breaks through and reveals what is necessary to overcome certain obstacles.

Our hopes are things that we believe should be. It was like Abraham. God spoke to him about having a son of promise. What happened? That son didn't arrive until he was 99 years old! I believe that because Abraham gave up his wife twice to other men that God needed to chastise him. God knew of His promise. The promise was still real but something had to change in Abraham's life before he was to find it fulfilled. God did not want a bad example for his son. In one sense, it is fruitless to discuss why Abraham had to wait so long. This is the way life turned out for him.

Perhaps it could have been shortened if he had made some positive changes earlier. He obviously did not see the connection between his sin and the lack of a child. He needed lots of time to change, and God gave it to him.

Holding onto one's hope

The great thing about Abraham is that he kept his faith in God that He would keep His promise. And in time God fulfilled His promise. His hope was greatly rewarded through the birth of Isaac and his descendants. The descendants of Isaac are still seen in the nation of Israel.

We do not always understand why our marriages do not improve more quickly. We should not be so quick to blame our partner. More often than not there is something from both sides that is malfunctioning. Our hope enables us to open our heart to God to bring us to higher standards in our marriage but in our own lives too! Hopefully it will happen before we reach 99 years old like Abraham! The most powerful hope verses in the scriptures are in Romans 4:18-21. They describe Abraham's persistent hope.

> *"In hope against hope he believed, in order that he might become a father of many nations, according to that which had been spoken, "So shall your descendants be." And without becoming weak in faith, he contemplated his own body, now as good as dead since he was about a hundred years old, and the deadness of Sarah's womb; yet, with respect to the promise of God, he did not waver in unbelief, but grew strong in faith, giving glory to God, and being fully assured that what He had promised, He was able also to perform."*

Behind this whole process is the assumption that God really wants to improve our marriages. He Himself works with us as He completes the restoration process. We should never forget the means God uses. The areas that we have already been blessed in are hopes fulfilled. Some wives take it for granted that their husbands seriously care for the needs of their home. They shouldn't. I can point out many men who spend their income on gambling or drugs.

A husband, on the other hand, should not

God is a God of miracles.

Change sometimes requires a long process.

Hope assures a persistent faith.

forget that God has already been working when he sees his wife faith-fully cooking meals for him and the family. This is becoming more and more rare as wives are influenced by the modern culture and live inde-pendent lives from their husbands.

Developing great marriages is a process. Each stage can be exciting and fun even though trials lurk around every corner. God desires to do many great things through your lives. Open the door of your heart and welcome Him into your marriage. Hope sets us on the right path lead-ing to His wonderful work of love and power in our personal lives and our marriages.

Chapter #1 Study Questions

1. From the best marriages you are acquainted with, list several key elements of 'great marriages?'

2. What are some signs of a spouse who has given up hope on his or her marriage?

3. Hope doesn't solve problems, but it
    "_____."

4. What are the major differences between the secular and biblical view of marriage?

5. Give one item of biblical support for the biblical view of marriage and explain.

6. Are non-Christians accountable to God for the way they treat their marriage? Why or why not?

7. Why are thoughts that lead to "giving up" on a good marriage always a form of temptation?

8. Make sure you have at least three or four items on your hope list for your marriage? Write them down.

9. How can looking at the areas of discontent in our marriages help us?

10. How do we know God designed marriage and it wasn't just man-made?

11. Why does God say that He created women?

12. Why were women so named?

13. Does the "oneness" God speaks of in Genesis 2 refer to the sexual union or more? Why?

14. Why do we ask you not to share your 'hope list' with your spouses unless they ask to see it?

15. What are two things we can learn about hope from Abraham in Romans 4:18-21?

16. Put a check mark here ☐ when you bring your hope list to the Lord in prayer. Develop a habit of praying this each day.

Building a
Great Marriage

#2 Unconditional Love: Life

Principle 1

A great building is built from a great blueprint. In the same way, great marriages are built according to God's glorious blueprint. Bad marriages do not result from an imperfect design but from builders who do not build according to God's plans!

There are two major dangers to be aware of. First, there are those who do not build according to the truth. They might profess to know the truth, but they simply don't build according to the instructions. Jesus had some hard words for these people "And everyone who hears these words of Mine, and does not act upon them, will be like a foolish man, who built his house upon the sand" (Matthew 7:26).

I have heard many spouses say they can't change. "That's just the way I am." It often really means, "I won't change." In other words, they know what is best but minimize or excuse the need to change. There is also another danger.

Bad marriages are aggravated by the fact that many people are convinced that their actions are according to the Lord's Word. They are not always correct. This kind of problem is even more difficult to overcome because pride is a factor. They do not welcome change.

So some do not want change while others have mistaken notions. In either case we are not to blame the design but the "builders" who ignore the blueprint. It is for this reason that we want to spend several chapters focusing on God's blueprint for marriage as revealed in His Word. The truths behind marriage are so powerful that they often make me weep when I think of them. You might wonder why. Let me explain the reason.

A) God's Design for Marriage

God created marriage not just to organize society and form happy families with children, but also to enable us to better understand the glorious truths of God.

When God decided to make a most wonderful relationship for mankind, He took the best model possible. Where was that found? It was found in the Godhead. When we investigate the design of marriage, we are peering into the heart of God. Paul speaks about this mystery in Ephesians,

> *"For this cause a man shall leave his father and mother, and shall cleave to his wife; and the two shall become one flesh. This mystery is great; but I am speaking with reference to Christ and the church" (Ephesians 5:31-32).*

Marriage is described as a mystery. Marriage is earthly, but it also is a picture of God's redemptive plan where we can observe God's great love.

God enables us to understand mysterious spiritual truths by better understanding earthly relationships. Here are three marriage analogies.

Three Marriage Analogies
(1) Christ left His heavenly Father
Husband leaves his father
(2) Christ secured a bride (with His life)
Husband secures a bride (with dowry)
(3) The church (His people) belongs to Christ
The wife belongs to her husband

God created marriage in order to fully reveal His love on earth. It is this mystery that Paul alludes to in chapter 5 of Ephesians. We will explore these wonderful plans here. There are three aspects we need to explore. We will first introduce the overall design and then address the first aspect of a great marriage. Now remember, these are holy truths. You might sense alarming moments as you look into these things of God. Don't be afraid. Let the truths of God speak to your heart. God desires to reveal the greater heavenly pattern to help us achieve better earthly marriages. We not only want to learn these truths but also carefully apply them to our lives so that we can have great marriages!

There are three life principles that make great marriages: (1) Unconditional Love, (2) Inner Fulfillment, and (3) Together Forever. Each is distinct but fully integrated with the others. The deeper we look into these truths, the more we see the beauty of God's redemptive plan working out His grace and goodness in our marriages. Let us now turn our attention to the first life principle: Unconditional Love.

B) Description of God's Love

The husband is to love his wife with God's love. God's love has several characteristics. If our love falls short of these qualities, then we should no longer call it love.[7] The apostle Paul uses the Greek word 'agape' to describes this special divinely impacted love in 1 Corinthians 13:4-7 and elsewhere in the New Testament.[8]

Love is patient, love is kind, and is not jealous;
love does not brag and is not arrogant,
does not act unbecomingly; it does not seek its own,
is not provoked, does not take into account a wrong suffered,
does not rejoice in unrighteousness, but rejoices with the truth;
bears all things, believes all things, hopes all things, endures all things.
Love never fails.

We readily admit that unless God is shaping our lives and thoughts, there is no way we will be able to consistently love our wives. Our pride, desires and society's pressures might induce us to act in a manner that seems loving, but these activities have shallow roots and cannot stand up to the real tests of life.

God's love is characterized by unconditional, no strings attached, acts of care. These loving acts are produced from a heart of love. The scriptures state that God's nature is love; "God is love." From that desire

---

[7] The development of love grows differently than we would expect. As we admit our failures to reach God's standards and confess our sins to God and those we have offended, God helps us grow in our love.

[8] See "God's Mighty Touch" to better understand 1 Corinthian 13's powerful message of love.

or perspective came forth a plan to extend that compassionate love into the world. This is what we know as His redemptive plan.

Uncondi- tional love

God sent Jesus Christ into the world to extend His love and compassion to rebellious sinners. We in no way deserved this kind favor. We do not, even for a moment, deserve His love to be extended to us. But God's love sent Christ to die on the cross to take away our sins.

"We love because He first loved us" (1 John 4:19).

In this example, we find that Christ totally devoted Himself to loving those who did not deserve it. His commitment did not depend on the reaction of God's people to Him, but on His determination to extend His love to the church in obedience to God the Father. So how would we describe agape love?

a) Unconditional

God's love is unconditional in the fullest sense of the word. His love is not dependent on any good found in us. It is not dependent upon any good thing He sees in us. Love rides on the back of grace. In fact, we are unable to properly respond to Him. Mankind is too absorbed in grabbing what it wants to recognize or respond to the Lord's love. When we translate this life principle to marriage, we realize that husbands, and men in general, need to live by principle rather than by feeling or circumstance. We do what we are called to do – regularly and constantly love our wives.

Unconditional, no strings attached love results in long-term marriages because it is not dependent on how a wife may respond to her husband at any given moment. It seems that the Lord has given husbands a special test during a wife's menstrual periods when wives often experience mood swings and skewed perceptions. Does our kindness vary during these times?

b) Compassionate

Compassionate love is only one way of describing God's tenderness, mercy, grace, kindness and goodness toward us in Christ. God did not send a Savior who performed great noble acts of love merely because of duty. Instead we find the Savior to be gentle, one who identified with our needs. Again, the husband's call is to extend the unequivocal goodness of God to our wives through our compassionate actions, thoughts, words and attitudes.

Husbands must go beyond providing food and shelter. These things are good. He might even make personal sacrifices for the home, but God's love will also shape his relationship with his wife. He will speak with kindness. He will have a gentle caring touch. He will be patient when misunderstood or even wrongly accused. Moreover, the husband will be sensitive to his wife's needs. He will engage her in conversation so that he can understand her. Christ's love was not detached but involved.

c) Devoted

God's love is also a devoted love. A devoted love reveals a priority of kind action despite the challenges and distractions of life. We see this devotion on the night before Jesus' death. "Father, if Thou art willing, remove this cup from Me; yet not My will, but Thine be done" (Luke 22:42).

Jesus asked if there was any other way to fulfill God's purpose. His highest priority was not to escape discomfort, displeasure, embarrassment, shame, sharp pain, rejection, mocking, injustice, and finally death, but to devotedly give Himself for the sake of His future bride, the church.[9]

Our devotion as husbands must be fixed and unchanging. By prioritizing our care for our wives even in view of possible danger or suffering, we reflect the devotion that God has toward us. Abraham did the opposite when he gave up his wife to the king. He was afraid that he would be killed so his beautiful wife could be taken. Our delight in our wives must not be focused on their beauty or joy in the relationship (though these things are nice), but on our commitment to care for them. This is what makes the wedding vow so powerful. The husband is making a commitment to be devoted to his wife whether in sickness or health, poverty or wealth.

I attended a memorial service of a good and faithful brother in the church. He set a wonderful example of faithfulness for our congregation. His wife, because of a disease, was not very coherent and needed assistance in her wheelchair. Each week he would bring her to church. He would carry her wheelchair up the church stairs and then assist her. Although he missed out on many opportunities to spend time with others, after his retirement he devoted himself to caring for her. This was God's devoted love given to a man to grant to his wife.

Our wives know when we are devoted to them because of our simple commitment to love them. This devoted love reveals itself in the way we set our short and long term priorities.

Summary

Husbands do not naturally have this unconditional, compassionate, and devoted love. This is only received by exposing our needy lives before the Living God. We must plead that His love will freely flow to our

---

[9] The example of Jesus shines in contrast to the feebleness of the disciples. Every last disciple turned aside from the possible negative consequences of being associated with Jesus. Scan Luke 22 to observe this.

wives through our feeble lives. We must confess that we cannot do this on our own, but we can and must follow through on our commitment to express this holy love. God can strengthen us.

I have personally discovered that the more I simply focus on my commitment to love my wife as Christ loved me, life becomes easier. I am better able to overcome other temptations because I am no longer deliberating over whether I should forgive or help out. I identify my purpose in life with loving my wife. Most of the raging battles that we experience are because we have not made this whole-hearted life commitment. Although you have taken your marriage vows, I recommend that you renew your commitment to love your wife as one of your main purposes in life. Do it without ceremony in your quiet time or when you sense your wife is misunderstanding you again.

The more husbands identify with this call to love our wives unconditionally, the more this love moves and stimulates our beings. Jesus taught that when we die to ourselves, then we begin to live. I have found this to be very true (though to be honest it takes a while to get used to this different orientation toward life and relationships). We first take steps of love and then the proper feelings and affections follow.

 God designed the husband to take the initiative in bringing a constant shower of unconditional love and kindness to his wife. God describes the husband's love as an uncompromising sacrifice in Ephesians 5:28.

"So husbands ought also to love their own wives as their own bodies. He who loves his own wife loves himself."

C) The Choice of Love

Love is the supreme choice. A man has two possible responses to God's love through Jesus Christ. He can accept or reject it. He can be influenced by God's love or shun it. If we embrace His love and determine to love, we love. When we refuse His love, then our response is shaped by our own will, desires, or social expectations and our hearts become hardened.

(1) The kinds of love

The Greek language has three words for our English word "love." Only "agape" love is a love that gives even when it gets nothing in return. Agape love responds to the responsibility to meet the needs of others regardless of the situation. What kind of love does your marriage run on?

The New Testament uses the Greek word *agape* to describe God's gracious love which in turn should drive the husband to consistently love his wife. He does not love everyone with that devotion. He commits himself to love his wife in the special context of marriage. The Greek word "eros" describes a passionate love often used in sexual contexts (note the derived English word 'erotic'). *Philia* on the other hand describes a trade-off love, "You are nice to me and so I am nice to you." We often see this kind of love happening in families and with friends.

3 Loves:	*Agape*	*Philia*	*Eros*
Description	Unconditional love	Social love	Passionate love
Mindset	Loves because of commitment	Loves as one is loved	Loves to get loved
Motivation	Motivated by God's command and other's need.	Motivated by expectations of others	Motivated by lusts and self-pleasure
Heart	Willing to make sacrifices	Tries to make an even trade-off	Willing to sacrifice others

Let's see how these different kinds of love shape our marriages. Marriages are built on three kinds of love:

1. **Marriage built on lust**
    The lust-oriented excitement that an *eros* marriage provides fades very quickly. Those who base their marriage on sexual excitement will soon look elsewhere for more excitement. This desire can lead men and women to do all sorts of things that they would never otherwise do. However, their excitement quickly wears off once the excitement passes. When offenses build up, it is no longer possible to have fun at home. They will look elsewhere for what they are pursuing.

2. **Marriage built on expected kindness**
    Philia love also wears thin quickly, but usually not as quickly as *eros* love. A husband loves his wife with the hope that she will return that

love. This works out nicely as long as each spouse is being kind to one another. The problem is that we are sinful creatures. The cycle turns negative when my spouse does not kindly respond to my good gestures. If my spouse is mean to me, should I return the meanness? Where does it end? If the way I respond to my spouse is dependent on how she treats me, then there will be a slow movement toward death. Because of our sin nature, we need a love that is not dependent on how the other person responds to us.

3.   **Marriage built on covenant love**
      Agape love (covenant love) agrees to love because of the commitment we make. We love because we are commanded to do so. Only God's love is sufficient for this. The source of love for *agape* love is God's love for us. Christ first loved us. He brought love into the world. The clearer the husband can commit himself to this sacrificial love, the stronger that love becomes. A deeper understanding of this love can also be seen in the Old Testament through the word, "lovingkindness" (Hebrew *hesed*). This is a covenant love. I love because I am committed to love.

(2) The need for love

Husbands are told to love because they are prone to live in self-oriented ways (we all are). Love is so necessary for the cultivation of a wife's glorious being. Love is the motivating power to treat others well no matter how that person responds to you.

In many cases it would seem that our wives do not at all deserve such kind acts. This is possibly true. But this is the age of grace not judgment. We are called to imitate Christ and refuse to stand in judgment over others including our wives. While judgment is God's duty, forgiveness is man's responsibility. We plead for grace to live out mercy and kindness. Our business and duty is to treat others as they ought to be treated because they are made in the image of God.

In marriage there are many, many opportunities to express this unconditional love. Sometimes it has to do with how one spends his free time. Does

> "*Beloved, let us love one another, for love is from God; and everyone who loves is born of God and knows God.*"
> *(1 John 4:7)*

he choose to spend a portion of that time with his wife interacting with her? Does he show his attraction for her by delighting himself in her? Opportunities to love abound. We must not think that the only place this love is expressed is in bed! Love requires us to always be sensitive to the needs of our wives.

(3) The test of love

Marriage becomes an excellent testing ground that reveals the sincerity and depth of love. Day after day, night after night, husbands are given opportunities to love their wives. Married life creates an intense situation within which the level of love can rapidly grow. We have many practical opportunities to display our love to our wives. The baby is crying and our wife is exhausted. We cheerfully stop what we are doing and pick up the baby. If we, however, turn away from our responsibility to love, then we will incite an evil cycle of bitterness that can overwhelm one's marriage. Hatred can rapidly increase if we are not purposeful in our love.

(4) The Source of Love

We do not naturally possess this kind of love. Self-love interferes with other-love. Examples of love can and should be understood from surrounding conditions like good parental example. Without Christ, we cannot love unconditionally. When a person becomes a Christian, God's love is implanted in their lives. As God's child, the husband is able to draw upon the strength and example of God to help him love his wife as Christ loved the church. This divine love is so essential to Christian living that God says if we do not have love, then we are not of Him.

"If someone says, "I love God," and hates his brother, he is a liar; for the one who does not love his brother whom he has seen, cannot love God whom he has not seen. And this commandment we have from Him, that the one who loves God should love his brother also" (1 John 4:20-21).

(5) Forgiveness & love

Love means we forgive. We cannot grant our wives forgiveness from God. Only God can do that. When a person does wrong to another, he becomes a moral debtor. He has held back the good and right action that was owed to the other person (in this case his/her spouse). As long as the debt stands between them, the relationship will incur all sorts of mistrust. But if we forgive, then we release the moral debt that person owes us. We can continue to develop trust in our relationships. We must choose not to take revenge but instead treat the other person with kindness.

- ❖ We forgive as Christ forgave.
- ❖ We accept as Christ accepted.
- ❖ We hope as Christ hoped.

(6) Patience and love

Love requires that we put aside our own preferences for the sake of another. How true this is in marriage. We pay close attention to what she or he likes. This means we patiently wait. It might mean we do not get the attention that we would like in the kitchen or the bedroom. We should gently communicate our needs to the one we love, but we must patiently encourage and train our wives to properly respond. While changes can come, deeper struggles are often behind the issues, and we need to be patient.

Our primary reason for being here is to love. If I can please my best friend, then I am happy indeed. Lust stains the very path it creates because it is focused on self. When selfish desires reign then there is no sensitivity except to one's own needs or wants! When our minds are working on how to better satisfy our own desires, we are figuring a way to obtain more! We are not thinking about how to give more.

Love is patient. Love means that sometimes we are not loved back. Loving means we sometimes have to wait a long time. Old Testament Law commanded that there be no marital relations during a wife's menstrual period or for a period after the birth of a baby.[10] Will you let your mind and body wander at this time? Or will you exercise self-control to show your loyal devotion to your wife?

"On the other hand, discipline yourself for the purpose of godliness; for bodily discipline is only of little profit, but godliness is profitable for all things, since it holds promise for the present life and also for the life to come" (1 Timothy 4:7-8).

Love exercises self-control because through it we can manifest God's love. In Christ we find all of the deepest and necessary strength for our lives to care compassionately for others, and especially for our own wives. This agape love nature is born from the new life that we gain through Christ when we are saved.

Summary

When we are driven by *agape* love, we are dedicated to distributing God's kindness to our wives. We trust God to take care of our own

---

[10] See Leviticus 12:1-6; 18:19; 20:18. We are not saying these laws are necessary for salvation. However, we wonder whether God has coded these laws to build good health practices into the lives of women. Perhaps they are instrumental in keeping women from miscarriages, yeast infections and help prevent the dangers of having children too quickly one after another.

needs and desires.[11] Our spouse might be tired, pregnant, mean, sick, or just plain distracted. We still seek to fulfill her special needs. We pray, help, encourage, buy flowers, etc. Our goal must not be to obtain sex but to focus on caring for our wives' special needs.

Personal Application

- There are three kinds of love. Do you respond to your spouse on the basis of his/her action (*philia*), personal reward (*eros*), or on calling (*agape*)? Evaluate which kind of love you live by in at least three different contexts when relating to your spouse (e.g. arriving home, getting up, evening, the bedroom, etc.).

- Your love best reveals itself in times of stress and testing. How do you respond to your spouse when things are not going well? Are your words kind and loving? Do you threaten? Again, think about what kind of love is in operation during those arguments. How does your action affect your communication? Give an example.

- Based on the questions above, observe areas in which you are not using agape love. Bring them to the Lord in prayer and if possible, speak calmly to your spouse about ways that you are seeking to grow.

D) Questions on Unconditional Love

There are many questions that arise when speaking about how unconditional love should practically work out in any given marriage. If these questions are not faced, they often become stumbling blocks. We justify living by a different kind of love which is not God's love at all. If we are going to be men who live out God's love in our marriage, then we must

---

[11] Sometimes trusting God with our needs expresses itself in desperate cries to God. Remember God is faithful. He will never bring you into a situation in which His grace is insufficient. See 1 Corinthians 10:13.

not allow any doubts to be used by the evil one to distract us from the commitment that God asks us to make.

1) What about the husband? How is he going to be fulfilled?

The question in long form is, "What if a husband devotedly loves his wife, and she simply doesn't fulfill his needs?" There is a fear that arises. If he loves and is not loved back, then what? He gives and gives but gains nothing. Perhaps in his worse moments he might even go further in his thinking, "God would not create such a terribly miserable situation, and if He by any chance does, I'm not going to be part of it."

When a person asks this question, he probably has a faith problem. If not properly handled, he will ultimately and selfishly withdraw from his marriage vows. He does not have enough faith in God to trust God's design. God has promised to care of a man as long as he obeys Him. Remember how Jesus had to trust the Father that His love on the cross would not be ineffective. As long as we demand love, we will never receive it! Below is a chart of how one's lack of faith turns into selfishness.

Lack of faith	Withdraw Commitment	Selfishness
He doesn't believe God's ways are ultimately the best despite the circumstances he finds himself in.	Because of his doubt, he holds back on his commitment	Because he cannot be sure of God's love and help, he uses his "love" as a means of getting love back. This then is no longer love!

2) Can I actually love if I am not being loved?

Modern psychology has instilled fear in those who have suffered its teaching. This view strongly states that if our basic needs are not being met, then we cannot care for another. This kind of "mental" reservation holds men back from the needed commitment of love. This path of thought becomes an easy excuse to indulge in one's lust. "If she is not going to satisfy me, then I need to satisfy my personal needs some other way." Although this observation might seem to make sense, it is contrary to God's rule. The reason for this is clear.

Men were designed to give. Husbands are made to give of themselves in love. By giving, God will take care of the needs of the husband. This is the power of love and faith. A husband's love is not dependent on his wife's response.

If a husband does not step out in faith to love, then he will step back in fear to lust. The command in the Bible for husbands to love their wives must overcome this fear. If we fear God more than any other thing, then we will obey God even if we have doubts about how a particular circumstance might work out.

I remember many a time secretly and quietly asking God to help me be patient with my wife. She was either not in the mood or going through a personal struggle. I brought my need to God. In most cases, within a day God in His own way miraculously strengthened her. I only needed to trust God in the matter. So fulfillment does not come first. Love comes first, even if I do not see how it will work out. This is devoted love.

3) Doesn't the wife need to love?!

After extensively hearing about the husband's responsibility to love his wife, the husband might begin getting concerned. In many cases, the husband is convinced that in order to improve the marriage the wife needs to change. So the husband asks, "What about the wife's obligation to love?"

First, we need to remember that even if our wives do not love us in return, our commitment to love them never changes. Of course, we all desire our wives to affectionately love us. This makes life so much more delightful. After all, we are building a great marriage, are we not? At different times, however, we might not receive this love back as expected (this is using the notion of *philia* love). We need to consciously engage in *agape* love. Without *agape* love we will never reach a great marriage. Every Christian can by God's amazing grace and power practically exude this love. Notice how the Apostle Paul instructs each Christian to engage in His privilege of loving one another.

> *"And so, as those who have been chosen of God, holy and beloved, put on a heart of compassion, kindness, humility, gentleness and patience; bearing with one another, and forgiving each other, whoever has a complaint against anyone; just as the Lord forgave you, so also should you. And beyond all these things put on love (agape), which is the perfect bond of unity" (Colossians 3:12-14).*

Second, there is a life truth from this teaching for all of us: men and women, single and married. We must not miss it. God established marriage so that all of us can familiarize ourselves with God's unconditional love.[12] The wife should not go away thinking that she need not love her husband. We understand from Jesus' teaching that we all ought to devotedly love one another. The truth is that everyone is called to love.

Men are challenged to a higher and more devoted love because of the intense and close marriage relationship. It is through this agape love that men can inject their marriage with God's amazing love. If we added

---

[12] In order to reach that love we often need to go through times of transformation. The Lord might use the wife we choose to chastise us. In other words, He uses difficult wives for difficult husbands. When sharpening a tool, a rougher instrument is needed to do the job. The final touching up requires a much more delicate tool.

a bit of blue coloring to some water, we would expect to see the water turn blue. The same is true with God's love. When we add agape love to our marriage, then we can in time expect to see a greater touch of the Lord's magnificent love.

4) Why are men so slow to follow Christ's example of God's love?

This is the more helpful question that we ought to ask as men. Men learn so slowly. The problem is that many of us have not been provided a good example from our fathers. The second problem is that we are often slow to prioritize the deepening of our relationship with God our Father. Through this relationship we can familiarize ourselves with God's great love by getting to know and obey Him more.

How many times does God have to specially provide help, guidance, strength and protection for us to be convinced of His love? Are we not forgetful, stubborn and unbelieving?! His love is based on principle and not what we deserve.

His giving has set love in motion on earth. The divine love of God through Christ is the sublime example of agape love that can greatly impact our cold hearts. Every husband is called to replicate this sacrificial love to his wife. Ephesians 5:33 says, "Nevertheless let each individual among you also (agape) love his own wife even as himself..."

The command to love is given to the husband so that even if he does not feel like loving, he still does love.

5) How does love relate to lust?

Since love is a ruling agent for all Christians, it is love that needs to shape a man's thoughts toward women in general. Agape love is shown not only in being patient so one can help an older person onto a bus but also in the way one thinks about other women. Women are not to be thought of in terms of how they can satisfy our sexual desires. No. That is our flesh with its passion.

The flesh runs contrary to the Spirit (see the end of Galatians 5). Love in this case means that we purposely refrain from thinking sexually about a woman that we are eyeing. God has reserved that woman for another man. He has not given that woman to us.[13] Love respects that. We stand back and simply pray for her future husband.

Even single men need to live by the principle of love rather than lust. Lust is built on getting and is the opposite of genuine love. Strengthening one's commitment to sexual purity is one of the ways a young man can develop God's love in his life. If you are to reflect God's love, then you must live a sexually pure life.

A side benefit develops when single young men choose to live a life of love. They can see much more clearly what kind of wife they ought to marry! They are not deceived by looks. They are looking for godly qualities. Note that if we do not train ourselves earlier, then we will need more "rough" training after marriage.

6) How does this command to love relate to a married man's sexual lusts?

In the end, the choice is between love and lust, or more clearly, between God and self. Marriage has helped us understand what kind of love we need to fight this war with lust. If we love, we will not lust. We will not like our lusts. We will be repulsed by their hideousness. However, if we neglect to choose love and the source of love (God), we will default to lusts.

---

[13] Here is a simple test. Ask yourself, "Would we be ashamed if others knew our true thoughts about another person?" When ruled by love, one only thinks what is good and lovely. If evil thoughts come, push them aside and choose to do even better things.

A great marriage tolerates no seductive pictures and movies. Why? They are fuel for the lust factory. Toleration of lustful thoughts reveals that one is not loving his wife. True love finds full contentment in a man's own wife. Our wives can get old. We are tempted to find satisfaction elsewhere. It is at this time we are to reawaken our commitment to agape love our wives (erotic love will fail).

Although we might think that our behavior is better now than before, we should not fool ourselves. A little less pornography or fewer lustful thoughts is not good enough! We do not look for improvements but rather eradication. Such imperfect improvements can lull us into dangerous waters.

> *When we love, let it be known there is no room for lust. But equally so, if we lust, then there is no love.*

7) What do I do when my wife doesn't think I love her?

Many marriages are not good. Mistrust has built up. This command from God for husbands to love their wives is the first huge step in the right direction toward improving one's relationship. After a time of selfishness, one's wife may be a little skeptical of your motives. She might not respond right away. This disbelief in your genuine love might even be further ruined through the way her father treated her mother. It will take time to reshape her thinking.

Don't be defensive and especially do not be offended (that would only convince her you do not love her!). Just continue to quietly love. Love unconditionally. Love forever. Love is going to be what rules your mind and thoughts from now on. But you can be sure, as a Christian, God

If you refuse to step ahead in faith to love LOVE FAITH then you will step back in fear to lust. LUST FEAR

is always willing to help you. Sacrifice might be required. Be willing to give and even to die in your love for your wife. This unconditional love is the heartbeat of a great marriage.

8) Can my love hold out?

There is a fear that steals away many a man's commitment. Some husbands demand to know "Can this kind of love last if I don't receive any encouragement back from my wife?" This person wants to have this kind of love but is not sure that he has all that he needs to properly carry it out. This question is good because it reminds us that our wife is not the source of our love. She might make our experience of loving her more exciting and enthralling, but once she becomes the source or strength of our love, then know for sure it will be short-lived.

People will always disappoint us. We must not make decisions according to how they respond to us. We must make the right decisions about how to act according to the truth of God's Word. Perhaps the real question is whether we can be sure of sufficient wisdom, strength, and love from God to meet the needs of the kinds of people we are expected to love.

True love and faith grow together. One cannot love unless one has great trust in God's design for marriage. He has to believe that God will somehow use our love to accomplish His greater purposes, even if it doesn't seem apparent at the point of crisis. Fear causes a man to forget about his commitment to his wife by turning his focus to self-pity. Now, let us focus on how to strengthen our *agape* love.

E) Source of Love: God's design of man

There are two sources for gaining this persistent love: 1) God's design and 2) God's calling.

God's Design of Man

The source of love comes through the knowledge of how God has designed us as men. Many of the doubts we have today are because we are no longer convinced that we are designed to love. In fact, for many men this is a new concept. It is much easier to be convinced by the world's talk as seen in ads where lust, alcohol or money are said to fulfill us. Emptiness comes from these things. They only entertain when one pursues them, but afterwards we know that these are not the things that fulfill us.

God's satisfaction comes when we accomplish His will. He gives us a strong sense of reward, encouragement, dignity, and renewed strength. It is fulfillment itself. There is always a sense of satisfaction when we are fulfilling the purpose God has for our lives. When it comes to the ability to love a grouchy, upset, and possibly frigid wife, we need to go back to our calling and design. This is what we are supposed to do. God made us for it. How does it work?

Love is the opposite of lust. Lust is only temporarily satisfied. And then it demands fulfillment again and again. Men brag, but did you ever hear anyone bragging about how badly they felt afterwards?! Not a chance. This is because guilt enters the scene.

Love is the opposite. Love is fulfilling even when we do not receive a nice response. Why? Love is a spiritual life principle built into the world and our lives. A person gains a sense of fulfillment merely by giving himself to another. The drive for love is giving. Giving up our own desires for the sake of another (even though not recognized) then provides more inner fuel for more love.

When I fix my gutters, I need to climb a 30+ foot ladder. Every time I come down I hope it is the last time I need to go up that ladder. How do I get up there without fear paralyzing me?

+ I see other men climbing tall ladders.

- ✦ I look at the instructions on the ladder that assure me the ladder can hold my weight.

- ✦ I also remember that I was up on that ladder before, and it held me up fine.

If I didn't have confidence in the ladder, I would leave it in its storage place. I would avoid that job at all costs. But confidence in the ladder's design enables me to do things that I would otherwise not do.

Great marriages are built by men who brave the unknown by trust in God's design for marriage. We don't have all the love that our lives will need at once. But more love comes as we again pour out love. Turned away? Be patient. Rejected? Love again. Turned back again? Keep loving. Criticized? Love endures.

Confidence in design

When does it end? When the situation is difficult, we look for an end to it. This is normal. Nobody likes such difficult hardships. We might hope for a sudden change that makes it easier. They sometimes come, but they are not solutions to a love that does not endure.

"Love bears all things, believes all things, hopes all things, endures all things. Love never fails" (1 Corinthians 13:7-8a).

As we endure in our love for our wives, we will see one of two possible things happen.[14] Because of our marriage covenant, we are committed to our wives no matter what.

Possibility #1 Break through

Ephesians 5 indicates that a husband's consistent love can melt down the distrust of his wife.

> *"Husbands, love your wives, just as Christ also loved the church and gave Himself up for her; that He might sanctify her, having cleansed her by the washing of water with the word,*
> *that He might present to Himself the church in all her glory, having no spot or wrinkle or any such thing; but that she should be holy and blameless" (Ephesians 5:25-27).*

God can use our consistent love to help strip away our wives' flaws. A husband's love is to be so constant that it wears down the dam of distrust. By God's grace, she slowly begins to understand what she never could before: genuine love. One day it will dawn on her, "Wow! My husband really does love me. So this is what love is really like."

Wives brought up with criticism or indifference, for example, have a difficult time believing someone truly loves them. She suspects her husband's motives. Only during times of crises, can a wife gain a glimpse of genuine love through her husband's persistent loving behavior. Her shell of distrust begins to soften. She begins to slowly understand how someone can truly love her just from devotion rather than from what he can gain from her. At that point she will begin to become increasingly receptive. A new sense of trust has been stirred. Her spots and wrinkles are slowly being ironed out. She responds to his gestures and words of love. More will be said about this in the next chapter.

---

[14] I am not prepared to say that God's love will always bring a breakthrough like we hope. Jesus had to die before He saw any lasting fruit from His love. His love, however, was never in vain and neither will ours be.

Possibility #2 Endurance

The second possibility is more difficult to accept. God is entrusting a few husbands with the opportunity to love their wives without seeing much, if any, change. It is much like a soldier who goes out to war. If he is primarily watching out for his own life rather than the lives of his buddies, then he makes a very poor soldier. Indeed, he is a threat to others. He cannot see how the ultimate goal of the war is more important than his own life. However, if he is willing to give his life for the sake of a greater good, then he becomes a brave soldier. Fears do not control him.

God has called me to brightly shine the torch of His love in your life.

Some might think this agape love is too much for God to ask of us. Why? We are a sissy generation of men. Bravery and courage are obscured by the darkness of selfish pleasure. We have no greater goals that call us beyond our immediate sensual pleasures. Agape love is far from our minds.

God, however, showed through His own more extreme example that He would ask His favorite subjects to replicate His love at great cost. God's own Son, Christ Jesus, was asked to love an obstinate people. This love saw no instant reward. His disciples fled from Him in His darkest hour. He even saw Peter deny Him. God, however, caused a greater good to come from His sacrificial love. The same will be true for us too. God always greatly uses agape love, even if we ourselves cannot see the results of it.

We cannot see the whole picture from this side of life, and we must not insist on seeing it. Some of us, like Hosea, will be asked to love under the most trying circumstances. His wife ran off several times prostituting herself to others. Others like Job will need to love their wives even during very testing times. Job lost his children and was plagued with a horrid disease. His wife did not support him during this ordeal.

Christ lived out love because it was the right thing to do, not because it was easy, quickly rewarded, or convenient. He was called to do it. Did God's people deserve it? Not at all. Husbands likewise are called and designed to sacrifice themselves for their wives through unconditional love for them. Each husband is called to offer that sacrifice of self like Christ our model. Every husband should love his wife with a lifelong love. This is sacrificial, unconditional *agape* love. There is no greater or nobler call than to love like Christ.

Summary

If we are going to run the race, then let us run to win. We need a picture of what it means when we cross the finish line. The Lord will come to us and say, "Good and faithful son, Well done!" We will be able to flash back through our lives to the times when we threw away our idols of self-indulgence and burned them in a sacrifice of self. We pledged ourselves to live according to His design for our lives no matter what the cost.

Any real and holy love for our wives should begin before we get married. In anticipation of giving your whole self to your wife, you must maintain purity in thought, word, and deed. Times of youth must be used to master self-control. The more vibrant this pre-marriage purity, the easier the 'distrust meltdown' can be addressed.

Choosing to love is our choice. We absolutely cannot love as God has designed without being close to Him. He has designed us to function this way. A choice to love is a choice to call upon God in His great and abundant mercies to seize our hearts with a selfless passion like His. Can there be a greater decision than to take our greatest joy in imitating God's love in this desperate world?! Definitely not.

As His men, we must make the calculated decision to spread God's amazing and powerful love to our wives and this world. I choose to constantly *agape* love my wife. Do you?

Men have been fooled by the world to think
that the greatest challenge is climbing some moun-
tain, shouting for a winning sport's team,
or chasing gorgeous girls.
God has, however, boldly stated that the greatest
challenge and joy for man is to unconditionally love
his wife.

A husband's pledge

"God has made me to love you my wife, truly and unselfishly. He has designed me so that every part of me can fully devote itself to you. I want your wedding dreams of that one man who will always only love you to come true. I am that faithful man for you.

At the very end of my earthly life, the Lord will know that I have been pure in my desire to wholly love you both before and during marriage. In faith I want to test the very foundational principles God has implanted in this universe when He made it. My mission will be to love you my wife as Christ has loved the church.

God has called me to brightly shine as the torch of His love in your life. Whether in poverty or wealth, youth or old age, in sickness or in health, I am determined to love you. Whether you, my dear, will be able to accept my love doesn't matter. I will constantly love and cherish you. I want my love for you to reflect Christ's love for His people. True love gives birth to great hopes."

Is there anything greater to live for?
Is there any more noble war to fight?
Is there any better race to win? No.

I was so designed to run,
and run I will by God's grace and power,
I will run the race of unconditional love for God and you.
May my all be for you, my love, my dear wife.

A prayer of the husband

"Dear Father in Heaven, I declare a holy war against pursuing my own needs. I have chosen the sure weapon of your enduring love. I have been designed to love. Away with infernal selfish pleasures that betray my loyalty to my God and wife! Away with each thought that would lead me into its condemned and greedy claws! Their time is gone.

I choose to love a pure love. I choose to live with a holy focus on my wife. I want with my love to penetrate the dark doors of death and confusion. With my constant and dedicated commitment to my wife I want to strip away all the fears and doubts that have been laid on her poor soul.

God fill me with your Spirit. Cleanse my soul of sin through Christ, for your calling is high and lofty. Grant that I may live fully devoted to my specially chosen woman. I have only one wife. I want only one wife. By your divine grace and example, I will give her and her alone my constant care as long as we both shall live.

And now, Lord I ask that you would protect what is so great and beautiful. Lift up what is glorious so that hope, joy, and love can again touch our miserable hearts. Let me join this race to run for your glory and nothing else. Lead me, Lord, with your precious example into a constant and flowing river of giving acts and words toward my wife. May I be pure, loyal, and responsible. And may the glorious love of God be revealed on earth in and through my love for my wife. By the grace and blood of Christ, God's only Son, I pray. Amen."

Personal Application

- Our hope for this lesson is that each man will commit himself to living by God's unconditional agape love, married or not. Read the pledge above aloud. Can you make it your own? Why or why not?

Pray through the prayer. Our hope is that by regularly repeating the prayer or pledge, you will refine it so it better fits your situation, tests and challenge.

- Wives, commit to pray for your husbands to arise to be these great men of God. Pray unceasingly for them. Imagine having a husband love you in this way? Do you like it? Then commit to pray for him. Write down a prayer if you need to, and when you see improvement in your husband, gently and romantically encourage him.

- Love not only shows itself during difficult times but each day of the year. One idea has helped couples better communicate their love to their partners. Have each spouse write down two ways that they feel loved. Also write down two ways that you think your spouse feels loved. Compare notes and discuss! (Read *Five Love Languages* by Gary Chapman for more insight).

Chapter #2 Study Questions

1. What is the first life principle for a great marriage?

2. List three words that describe this principle.

3. Have you taken steps to live by the principle of love? How so?

4. Have you felt cheated by following the path of lust? Explain.

5. Do you feel you deserve God's love? Why or why not?

6. Share an incident that reminds you of an experience of God's love.

7. What are the three Greek words for love? How does each shape a marriage?

8. Why must love forgive? Have you completely forgiven your spouse?

9. What about the situation where a husband is not fulfilled? What should he do?

10. How do love and lust relate to each other?

11. What should we tell the husband who says he cannot sustain his love?

12. How does God help sanctify a wife through a husband's faithful love?

13. What should you do if your wife refuses to respond to your love? For how long?

14. Have you as a husband renewed or made that commitment to un-
    conditionally love your wife? If not, why not? If so, sign your
    name and date it here.

Building a
Great Marriage

#3 Humble Submission: Life Principle 2

God has provided a way to have great marriages. His design is fully trustworthy. Marriage is much like a ship trying to enter a harbor on a stormy night. Everything is guesswork. Mistakes are fatal. We see marriages failing all around us. Even those with reasonably good marriages fear that some unknown flaw will become apparent and devastate their marriage. We must not only resist living in fear but also choose to live by faith in God's great design for marriage. God's design is fully trustworthy.

"Where you tend a rose, my lad,

A thistle cannot grow."[15]

---

[15] By Frances H Burnett in "The Secret Garden." As we live by faith, fears cannot lay hold of our lives. Thistles are undesirable plants.

When we trust in God's design, we are in fact putting our faith in God Himself. This faith is not only sufficient for our own lives but also for the many suffering couples around us that are desperately seeking help. God wants us to live in hope. When that lighthouse beams shine, suddenly the captain of a ship knows to stay to the south of the light to sail into the safety of the harbor. Putting our trust in God's design for marriage is like being safely guided by that light.

God's marriage design is fully trustworthy. First we need to learn how God's design works and then put it into operation in our lives. In this chapter we will look at the second life principle of 'Humble Submission.' We use this phrase 'life principle' to describe something that though specifically applicable to a situation like marriage, is also needed for godly living.

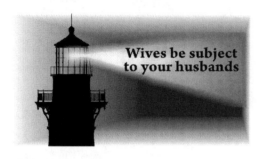

Wives be subject to your husbands

The first life principle of 'Unconditional Love' evokes the question: "Why isn't the wife also commanded to love?" Wives also ought to love their husbands. That is understood. Everyone is accountable to love others. But for husbands, the command to love stands out as the beacon from the lighthouse.

Husbands don't need a lot of beacon lights or commands to bring help to their marriage. Like a technician, God knows what part needs fixing or replaced. His counsel is straightforward. Wives don't need this command to love in the same way (even though wives too can be selfish), though they generally are called to be loving in all that they think, say, and do. Women are made differently and relate differently to their spouses. Their beam from the lighthouse says,

"Wives, be subject to your husbands as to the Lord"
(Eph 5:22).

This one command helps wives during their many confusing moments. When darkness revolves around her soul and all sorts of voices shout what she ought to do, God's clear light brings the needed direction. Through this simple and straightforward command God brings help to a wife during these times. We need to learn more how this one short direction can help her even in her dark moments. When wives submit themselves to their husbands, they remember their calling and find rich fulfillment.

A) Understanding the Second Life Principle: Humble Submission

Marriage can seem extremely complicated because of insurmountable marriage problems that people face. God doesn't want us to be overwhelmed. The solution is within reach. In fact, God has given us a picture lesson so that we can easily access what we need to know even at the most bewildering times.

The design of marriage is modeled after God's own redemptive plan that is reflected in His own person. The scriptures call the parallel between Christ and the church and the husband and wife a solved mystery.[16] In other words, Christ's coming

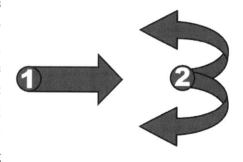

---

[16] The word 'mystery' in the New Testament refers to a solved mystery, something that before was incomprehensible. Now with further revelation, the mystery is revealed as in this case.

and displaying God's love for His people has unlocked the truths of marriage.

The earthly image of marriage can help us better understand these spiritual truths. Sometimes though, especially for those that grew up in broken or troubled homes, it is spiritual truth that helps them better understand how to improve their own marriages.

The gospel mystery was first revealed when God sent His Son Christ to die for our sins. God loved us, the church, even though we did not love Him. The cross was necessary for our sins to be forgiven so that we could be reconciled to Him. This is God's great love. This unconditional love is the first life principle that must shape a husband's love for his wife. The scriptures speak very clearly of this love in Ephesians chapter one.

> *"In Him we have redemption through His blood,*
>
> *the forgiveness of our trespasses,*
>
> *according to the riches of His grace which*
>
> *He lavished upon us."*
>
> *(Ephesians 1:7-8a)*

He loved us, chose us, sacrificially bought us so that we could belong to Him and share in His vast glory throughout all eternity. This is the real love of God that floods and radiates our souls even when no one else loves us. His love satisfies all of our deepest longings. We are able to perfectly respond to our mates because His love fills us even when our spouse is unfaithful. But the mystery doesn't stop there.

While the husband is to imitate God's love for the church, the wife is to emulate the church's response to her Lord Jesus Christ. As the church faithfully responds to the Lord's directions, so the wife is to follow her husband's directions. "But as the church is subject to Christ, so also the wives ought to be to their husbands in everything" (Ephesians 5:24).

+ Loved
+ Chosen
+ Bought
+ Belonging
+ Share

The church is awed that God would ever love her. She was an undesirable outcast. And yet, our majestic Lord purchased His people so that they could become part of His glorious redemptive plan and share in His eternal riches. As the church focuses on her inherent undesirability, and yet her grand position, she is able to gain a new perspective of her life.

She is delighted and eager to be faithful and obedient to her Lord. In the same way a wife should take joy in being chosen by her husband to be his bride and live out her life and commitment. In her honored position, she delightfully does anything to be with him. She is eager to submit to his every word and whim. She finds fulfillment in that special position of serving her husband. There is one more aspect of this mystery.

God has a purpose in His love. He has a purpose for His people. Oftentimes the wife becomes disillusioned with housework, caring for crying babies, wiping snotty noses, demands on her limited time and energy, etc. She needs to think back to God's purpose for obtaining His bride. We see this in the following verses.

> *"In order that in the ages to come He might show the surpassing riches of His grace in kindness toward us in Christ Jesus. For by grace you have been saved through faith; and that not of yourselves, it is the gift of God; not as a result of works, that no one should boast. For we are His workmanship, created in Christ Jesus for good works, which God prepared beforehand, that we should walk in them"* (Ephesians 2:7-10).

God's plan for the church is to bring His surpassing riches to His people. At the same time, however, He has instructed us that in order to obtain these riches we must do good works. It isn't impossible. God has already planned them out for us. We just need to follow through in the power of His Spirit and grace. What would you say about God's inten-

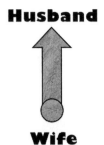

Husband

Wife

This is God's design.

tion? Is He not more than good? He surely is. As His people, therefore, we eagerly carry out these good works. This is our opportunity to complete Christ's good works. We serve Him while we serve others.

Nothing has changed when we think of the wife's need to subject herself to her husband. This is her calling. This is her opportunity for good works. She just needs to do it. It is a matter of obedience. When she carefully lives out God's love through her service, she impacts her husband, children and the world.

"Her children rise up and bless her;
Her husband also, and he praises her, saying:
"Many daughters have done nobly, but you excel them all"
(Proverbs 31:28-29).

We see then that God's plan is for women being liberated, not revolting as some would react to God's command. Submission is the wife's means to expand God's kingdom of love. Many have questioned the Lord's intention in calling the woman to submit to her husband. These suggestions breed all sorts of revulsion to Christ's command. Clearly, this is not what the Lord intended. He paved a path of gold and called her to walk on it beside Him. At the end of the path is the castle.

We need to better understand why the Lord gave this command to wives. This will help sort out many misunderstandings about a woman's function and enable her to further commit herself to it.

B) THE TWO CHOICES

The wife will soon learn that though the pathway is clearly laid out there is a tremendous amount of inner turmoil about walking on that path. She will need to make a clear choice: either following her feelings or following the scriptures. Actually, in order to do a fine job, she will need to clearly acknowledge several truths:

+ She will subject herself to her husband in everything. (Ephesians 5:24).

+ She will seek her husband's guidance on what and how to do things.

+ She will find inner satisfaction primarily from God's own love for her as His child.

+ She will trust the Lord as her ultimate Protector and Provider.

The secular world has taken hold of the media, and the average wife hears much more from the world than from God. She needs to clearly understand that the world has persuaded her or is attempting to do so.

The scripture states that true satisfaction will come when she denies her own choices and sets her heart on pleasing her husband. The more she affirms that this is what she is designed and called to do, the more she will receive a wonderful extra zeal and a touch from the Lord to help her be that great helpmate. Wives, or wives-to-be, need to be wary of the evil one's strong voice blasted through the world's loudspeakers or she will feel that she is being cheated out of the supposedly 'good' life.

Fulfillment through rebellion

The wife is being tempted all the time to deny the authority that God has placed over her. This happened in the Garden of Eden when Eve heard a clever voice calling her to 'freedom' or 'independence.'

"When the woman saw that the tree was good for food, and that it was a delight to the eyes, and that the tree was desirable to make [one] wise,

she took from its fruit and ate; and she gave also to her husband with her, and he ate." (Genesis 3:6)

Since that temptation had such good effect, Satan still uses the same mode of attack today! Satan starts by subtly questioning the goodness of God's will. The serpent suggested that Eve was missing out on something better, that God was withholding something better from her.

> (1) Satan questions God's good will.
>
> (2) He suggests that she is missing out on something better.
>
> (3) He draws her mind away from God's command to something that promises to satisfy.
>
> (4) Satan snag's her allegiance by persuading her to obey what he says.

Then Satan draws her mind away from God to something that pleases her. Lastly, he attempts to snag her by enticing her to obey him. This last point is important.

By doing something different than the Lord clearly stated, she is actually coming out from under the authority of her husband and placing herself under the authority of another. The scripture says that Eve was deceived. In her deceived frame of mind she believed that her opinion was better than obeying God. Now let me ask, "Is it not true that wives are often tempted, by thoughts and feelings, to do what they feel is right rather than what their husbands ask them to do?"

Without being constantly aware of the truths of God, the woman will be caught off guard and begin making decisions according to her own opinion. Because this is so common, perhaps it would be good to face some of the subtle arguments that the world uses to brainwash women.

C) Subtle Arguments

Argument #1: Husband and wife should keep their independence

Husbands and wives today often think of marriage more like a business contract where they share resources together. These husbands and wives think that they are better off, having two independent lifestyles, sometimes due to fear that things might not work out too well. See the illustration on the right.

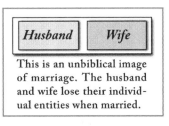

This is an unbiblical image of marriage. The husband and wife lose their individual entities when married.

This kind of marriage looks intact because the couple lives with each other (sometimes even this is not so!). That might seem like oneness, but it is not a picture of biblical marriage. In this case one could theoretically have two males or two females. They both have their own jobs and their own lives. Marriage in these terms is a mere social contract that guides how they conduct their common affairs. Because of this perspective, they are subtly readying themselves for the possibility of divorce. In their minds, divorce is only canceling a human contract much like a rental contract. "It just didn't work out."

This illustration better displays the marriage effect of oneness. They are complements of each other.

The illustration on the left portrays the integration or interdependence of the husband and wife. Their identities are distinct and yet intertwined through the covenant before God. They complement each other. They need each other; together they are one. This is the reason Jesus said,

"And the two shall become one flesh; consequently they are no longer two, but one flesh. What therefore God has joined together, let no man separate" (Mark 10:8-9).

The wife is not pictured as an independent unit. The husband and wife are integrated together much like two gears. As the husband 'turns', so the wife 'turns'. Another graphic helps us gain a biblical perspective of marriage.

The illustration on the right demonstrates this male-female integration within the marriage. As the dominant (husband) initiates, the female (wife) responds.  **This even better illustrates the oneness of the married couple.**

Both are needed to form a whole. "They are no longer two but one flesh," No image perfectly represents this union, but each in its own way helps us to better understand and appreciate God's design.

The husband is often portrayed as foolish and selfish. The wife is to draw the conclusion that if she has any sense, she should not let him make any decisions that affect her. But this counsel is godless. This view places no weight on the design of marriage, the responsibility of the wife before God or what God desires. In fact, her response should be dictated by God's overriding command, not her husband's ability to lead well.

Argument #2: Protection for Self and Family

The reason that many reject the wife's need to submit to her husband is for the protection of both herself and her children. The assumption of this argument is that God does not help or protect the needy wife and children. The wife believes that she can best protect herself. This is because false beliefs have entered her mind. "God doesn't care for us." "God can't help us."

The God of the scriptures is righteous. He is very much concerned with all forms of oppression and will properly judge these in

This is waywardness.

His time. We see this in the scriptures where the true Christian displays his heart by caring about the needs of women and children because they are often oppressed or found in difficult straits.[17]

God, however, also sees the heart. He sees that another issue lies behind a wife's willingness to excuse her lack of submissiveness by taking things into her own hands. God is not blind to the abuse happening. He is more familiar with it than any of us. However, if we refuse to face the real reason women reject God's command, our solutions will lead us off course. Greater problems will occur. The need for a steady faith in a just God is very apparent.

Argument #3: Submissiveness allows men to trample upon women

Unfortunately, women have been treated as less than persons in the past and present. This certainly is not the perspective we get when we look at how God designed women. But when people refuse to believe the scriptures, all sorts of distorted views result. Women are of great value to God. They hold a great part of God's overall purpose for mankind.

From the promise of Genesis 3:15 we find that God uses the woman to bring deliverance into the world. Where would Moses have been without the faith of his mother? Where would Jesus be without the faith of Mary? The whole book of Ruth is built around how the faithfulness of one woman enabled the Messiah's line to continue on.

As mentioned before, submissiveness is simply the proper thing for a wife to do. This is God's calling for her. This is not to deny any of her

---

[17] James 1:27 say, "This is pure and undefiled religion in the sight of our God and Father, to visit orphans and widows in their distress..."

gifts or abilities. This is one of her gifts and opportunities. She is assigned to complete the husband because she is specially designed for it. The Lord has designed her gifts to function best by complementing her husband's leadership.

The world has stained the word "submit" or "be subject to," but subjection plays an important role in everyone's life. Society couldn't function without it. The chart below shows various ways this same Greek word "to be subject to"[18] is used in the Bible.

All things to Christ	And when all things are **subjected** to Him, then the Son Himself also will be **subjected** to the One who **subjected** all things to Him... (1 Corinthians 15:28).
Slaves to their masters	Urge bondslaves to be **subject** to their own masters in everything, to be well-pleasing, not argumentative (Titus 2:9).
Younger to their elders	You younger men, likewise, be **subject** to your elders (1 Peter 5:5).
Churches to Christ	But as the church is **subject** to Christ. (Ephesians 5:24).
People to rulers	Remind them to be **subject** to rulers, to authorities, to be obedient, to be ready for every good deed (Titus 3:1).
Wives to their husbands	To be sensible, pure, workers at home, kind, being **subject** to their own husbands, that the word of God may not be dishonored (Titus 2:5).

---

[18] This Greek word clearly means to obey instructions in an authoritarian context. A general, for example, expects his soldiers to completely follow his orders.

In the end, everyone will submit to God. If we choose to humble ourselves now, we are promised a great reward. If we are stubborn and refuse to submit to our authorities, then indeed we are readying ourselves for judgment. Although there is no guarantee that the husband will get better, the wife that subjects herself to him can have full confidence that God is overseeing the situation.

Obedience produces the best situation possible – not the worst as alleged! Fulfillment comes from submission, not from wrestling leadership away from the husband.

Argument #4: Submission is equal to suffering

Some people strongly object to the requirement for a wife to be submissive to her husband because they assume that it is the same as suffering. Those with bad experiences cannot even think that a marriage with submission could be a good thing. We are sorry that so many women have borne such pain from abusive husbands. When lust rules over love, mean selfishness steps upon the lives of others. Abuse occurs. This is the result of sin, and until the Lord returns, it will unfortunately be present.

Wives need to remember that in taking matters into their own hands there lies a greater danger. This is all too evident in all of the crazy judgments being issued from the family courts. Women have not won when they lose their husbands. When a wife chooses not to obey her husband she suffers, her children suffer and society suffers as well.[19] The hardening of a woman's heart basically shuts off any hope for change and improvement.

We have probably all seen a family destroyed by a husband's foolish behavior, whether associated with alcoholism, drugs, quest for fame, or just plain immorality. We agree that the husband's love is not perfect on

---

[19] Tragic results include declining populations, lonely old people, latch-key children, adultery, divorce and general distrust in marriage. This is worse than a bomb for in these cases people live dismal lonely lives.

earth. Sometimes we see something totally opposite to what it should be. But this does not mean the wife is excused from submission. In these cases, the wife will need to put her trust in God to care for her and her family's needs.

"In the same way, you wives, be submissive to your own husbands so that even if any of them are disobedient to the word, they may be won without a word by the behavior of their wives, as they observe your chaste and respectful behavior" (1 Peter 3:1-2).

By trusting God and being a faithful wife, the wife is responding to God's great love and mercy. This hope in God becomes a powerful tool to bring forth extra grace and love from God. The same principle is used in a more general way for those who are being mistreated by others because of righteousness. They are to keep doing right and trust God. (Read the rest of I Peter chapter 3).

Many people hold to unbiblical positions about suffering. These difficult situations are opportunities for God's people to openly serve God and bring testimony to those around them. Jesus said this so clearly,

"Blessed are those who have been persecuted for the sake of righteousness, for theirs is the kingdom of heaven. Blessed are you when men cast insults at you, and persecute you, and say all kinds of evil against you falsely, on account of Me. Rejoice, and be glad, for your reward in heaven is great, for so they persecuted the prophets who were before you" (Matthew 5:10-12).

Persecution, insults, and false accusations are not light matters. We cannot insist that our lives be free from suffering. These most difficult situations provide the greatest opportunities to display God's love and to possess greater virtue on earth and rewards in heaven. Both men and woman must find their joy in the Lord during such times of suffering. God sees and will richly reward them for their faithfulness in the most stressful and difficult times. Could anything that happens to us be worse than what our Heavenly Father permitted to be done to His only son Jesus Christ? No. We need to eliminate loopholes for our sins.[20]

D) The Importance of Submission to the Maturing Process

Most arguments about the submissiveness of the wife are negative. We must, however, see that God accomplishes great things through the faithful wife. Mary was a beautiful example of this when she accepted the Lord's words. We will focus on heart changes.

Those that choose to disobey will grow in their fears. When a person, however, repeatedly takes steps of obedience, that person begins to develop trust. Let's look at these two processes.

Fear's Impact

Everyone needs to mature. Fear and doubt, however, destroy the growing process. Fear strips away the trust that is needed to take steps of faith. If I fear something bad might happen to me when I go to the store, then I probably won't go there. I have no faith that the good I want to happen will occur.

If a wife has no faith that being subject to her husband will do her any good, then she will not submit to him. The elderly church leader John connects love and fear in this way.

"There is no fear in love;

but perfect love casts out fear,

because fear involves punishment,

---

[20] The greatest problem of suffering is man's dedication to the idol of pleasure. People tend to worship God only when it is easy. Pleasure is their idol.

and the one who fears is not perfected in love." (1 John 4:18)

Love cannot exist as long as fear is present. Love requires faith and trust. As long as worldly arguments heavily influence the mind of the wife, she simply will not subject herself to her husband during difficult times. She will be afraid that worse things will happen. She cannot fathom how God would be able to express His love and kindness to her in such times. And so the worsening cycle continues to unravel and reveal its destructive head.

This is what happened at Kadesh-Barnea (see sidebar). God had every good intention, but the Jews grumbled. One of the arguments in their minds went like this, "Because the LORD hates us...." That attitude is fatal.

Once we question God's motive, our faith is paralyzed. We have stepped back to the Garden with Eve. In such cases there is no choice but to retreat to doubt and despair. A rejection of God's Word and disobedience follow. Eventually, these lead us to horrible consequences. Fear simply does not allow relationships to grow. Fear undermines the trust that is necessary for growth.

> **Crisis at Kadesh Barnea**
>
> "Yet you were not willing to go up, but rebelled against the command of the LORD your God; and you grumbled in your tents and said, 'Because the LORD hates us, He has brought us out of the land of Egypt to deliver us into the hand of the Amorites to destroy us" (Deut 1:26-27)
>
> God's love → Doubt His love → Reject His word → Respond to fear → Disobey → Problems develop → Distance from Lord

Faith's Impact

On the other hand, when we simply obey, our trust is able to grow. Remember, marriage is God's perfect design. It doesn't have any flaws. God Himself is fully trustworthy. So when we put our trust in God, we will be led along a road which will strengthen our trust. We must acknowledge that this road is not predictable in where it might take us or how long we might need to travel in one direction or another, but if we hang

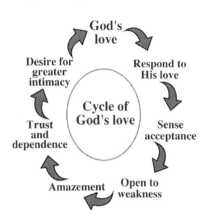

on tight we will end up at the right place. This is important for wives who must regularly trust God to watch over their heart concerns such as for their children.

The love of God gives us a special desire to please God. This motivates us to take steps of obedience, although they run contrary to what we might feel. This submissiveness, then, actually is a step of faith. Wives don't know specifically how things will work out. They only know God is faithful who made the promises to His obedient children.

The agape love of her husband will also move the wife to a more complete obedience. She wants to please him. She finds she doesn't need to contest him anymore because she can trust him to make the best judgment.[21] Love melts fears and doubts away. Even if she doesn't find the perfect love she would like from her husband, she can still find it in God's love for her. This faith then enables her to take the daring steps of being subject to her husband in love. One can see that if there is any hope for a good relationship, it will need to be restored through steps of trust and love. The wife's submission is a critical aspect of this growing relationship.

---

[21] This does not mean that the husband should ignore the insight that comes through his wife. A man is foolish to ignore the things he can learn through his wife. She is his helpmate. He needs her. It is important to reach the right balance where the husband is leading but valuing her input.

Our ability to love comes from being loved and accepted. There is a great and deep security that is brought about when we are perpetually and unconditionally loved. This unconditional acceptance leads to openness and humility in our lives. Fears and doubts can be put aside. As we do this, we are further amazed at His great love for us. We do not need to impress God to gain His favor. Trust is built up. We want to experientially know God at a deeper level. This seeking of God then brings us to know God and His love on a deeper level.

Fulfillment by a growing trust

In a great marriage, each spouse is looking to God to meet their needs. Every problem is an opportunity to trust God for a solution. Trust enables the wife to put aside her fears one by one. Instead of being rigid and hardened, her face becomes increasingly calm and soft.

Just as the warm spring sun causes flowers to open wide in their brilliant glory, a husband's consistent agape love breaks away those reserved fears that hold back her total trust.

Her budding trust enables special growth to occur within the marriage relationship. The command for wives to subject themselves to their husbands directs them into the best life possible. Obedience leads to trust and love.

> "So the LORD commanded us to observe all these statutes, to fear the LORD our God for our good always and for our survival, as it is today. And it will be righteousness for us if we are careful to observe all this commandment before the LORD our God, just as He commanded us" (Deuteronomy 6:24-25).

The husband is called, like the sun, to produce a strong beam of love upon his wife. Through this love her confidence in his love is deepened and her life fulfilled. Furthermore, when her husband devotedly loves her, she becomes a very satisfied woman full of God's love and glory ready to love any one. Have you ever met such a woman? Would you want to be such a woman? Why not pray and ask God to make you like a radiant flower exuding God's love.

E) What does Christian submission look like?

Some wives want to get a better picture of what this submission looks like in a marriage. There are numerous illustrations and instructions that help us to do that very thing.

A genuine but powerful love will blossom in the woman with a quiet and submissive heart. Her roughness becomes tenderness. This is what makes women genuinely beautiful. Observe what the apostle says below.

And let not your adornment be merely external--braiding the hair, and wearing gold jewelry, or putting on dresses; but let it be the hidden person of the heart, with the imperishable quality of a gentle and quiet spirit, which is precious in the sight of God" (1 Peter 3:3-4).

A) A Wife's Tender Response	B) A Wife's Quiet Response
As long as there is competition or contention, the man will naturally struggle to win the argument.	As long as the wife reproves or openly attempts to correct, the husband will ignore common conversation.
A gentle heart enables the man to retire from his fighting mode, enjoy his wife's company and value her person and thoughts.	Her quiet spirit encourages the husband who tends to talk less to speak and share his heart. It is here that she builds him up.

Numerous questions arise when a wife begins to think about how to practically submit. For some it is a shock. One wife might be thinking of how absolutely evil her husband is. Should she still submit to him? Yes, (unless he tells her to do evil with or for him).

Another wife might be wondering if it is possible to subject herself to such an evil husband. God gave us a picture allowing us to see that it is possible and good to do this very thing. An Old Testament figure named Abigail was a faithful wife. She faithfully endured an evil husband. God finally took his life. David then praised her discernment.

A woman's fulfillment should not be dependent on her husband exercise of unconditional love just as a husband's love should not be dependent upon the wife's submissive response. This enables the wife to rise above her circumstances to devotedly serve her husband even when he is a 'crumb.'

Another key example of this same matter is Sarah. She certainly did not get her motivation to comply with her husband's wishes from how he treated her! He pawned her off to other men to protect his own skin! Her holy decision to do what he asked made her a wonderful woman.[22] She gave herself to the Lord, and the Lord intervened and protected her both two times Abraham did this.

"For in this way in former times the holy women also, who hoped in God, used to adorn themselves, being submissive to their own husbands. Thus Sarah obeyed Abraham, calling him lord, and you have become her children if you do what is right without being frightened by any fear" (1 Peter 3:5-6).

---

[22] Perhaps it is because of cultural differences that I have a great deal of difficulty accepting Sarah's decision as proper. If it weren't for the 1 Peter 3 passage and the way that the Lord intervened, it would seem improper to give herself to these men. But perhaps, and this is how I resolve it, she would have told the men if they had made any real advances upon her.

Ideally, a man would faithfully love his wife and the wife would open her heart to her husband by being submissive to him. They should function as one, fully complementing each other. Our world, however, is not ideal. Our spouses will not live in complete harmony with God's will. But even in these situations, or even in a worst case scenario, when a husband is not being faithful, the wife who is dependent upon God can still faithfully subject herself to him.

> *"(Now the man's name was Nabal, and his wife's name was Abigail. And the woman was intelligent and beautiful in appearance, but the man was harsh and evil in his dealings, and he was a Calebite)"* (1 Samuel 25:3).

Women are not to be haughty but humble. They should not erroneously think that men can do anything that they want while she is 'locked up in the home.' We are all servants of the Almighty God. Men must focus on listening to and obeying God. The man's position is different than his wife's, but the opportunity to obey the Lord is the same. Humility will not presume a position higher than what God has allotted us. Position and calling are closely associated and found in the way God has made us.

There is no room in a marriage for two lords. If a couple is to harmoniously work together, then one must stand as leader and the other as follower. The church's blessing increases as she lovingly responds to Jesus Christ her bridegroom. God is just waiting for us to respond in obedience so that His powerful love will more deeply empower us to live as Christ did.

When a couple gets serious about building a great marriage, God will enable the husband and wife to work closely together. They will continually interrelate and thus grow in their relationship. Much of this growth comes from deep conversation with each other. If the husband and wife are not talking and sharing, then there is much less opportunity for growth.[23]

How much have you as a couple shared heart issues? Do you regularly pray together for each other? My wife and I have been discussing things and praying together every night for over thirty years. Yes, it has cost us. No time for late night television, movies or browsing. But it is during these times that we can help each other. I put it this way. Would you rather argue and feel upset or wisely plan out your time?

Summary

In the security of God's love, wives can grow in their trust in Him to help them brave those difficult situations requiring submission. These faith choices foster better marriages in which a wife finds ever greater fulfillment from her husband who increasingly considers her a special part of his life.

---

[23] This happens too in a spiritual sense when we neglect to meet with the Lord in daily devotions where we pray to God. From this we see how important it is for the husband and wife to enter healthy dialogue with each other. Good working relationships depend on good communication.

F) Questions about Submission

There are many important questions that are asked. Let's look at a few of them.

What if a wife is not loved by her husband?

If a wife does not have this perfect love from her husband, she is still responsible to respect and submit to him.[24] This is God's calling and design for her. How is she able to do this?

She is able to live out a quiet submissive spirit to her husband through the way God meets her deepest needs. When God satisfies the deepest part of the life of a woman, then her deepest and most basic needs are cared for. She then has strength to trust God to watch over her in a difficult marriage. She can trust Him to fill her heart with divine love and humility.

Can a wife be overly submissive?

A wife cannot be overly submissive if she properly understands what submissiveness means. First, it does not mean that she is a soulless creature delivering a newspaper to her master. Think back to Adam's original response to Eve. Think about the woman in Proverbs 31. A woman is an alive and dynamic creature created to fulfill special needs in a man so God's greater purposes can be done through her. A woman must see this as her life calling and not just some small part of her life. She must only submit "in the Lord" which should be interpreted to mean that she should not do what would not please the Lord.

Shouldn't a husband love his wife?

A husband definitely should love his wife. He has covenanted to do this. But whenever the wife demands this love, she reveals a hardened heart which repulses the man. She is trying to manipulate him into meeting

---

[24] Women and their parents should discern a husband's consistent love before marriage! Afterwards, it is too late to change.

her needs. Isn't this the opposite of what should be happening? Shouldn't she be trying to see his needs and meet them? She only uses this, "If you loved me, then you would ..." argument to control him. This is ungodly behavior filled with selfishness.

She needs to meet with God so that He can meet those needs. She then has the reserves to subject herself to her husband. Husbands detest demanding wives. They don't have the time or the energy to meet an unending list of commands. Only God can fulfill those needs. A husband is no substitute for God. Such demanding women need to be touched by God's love.

How should I respond when I feel so strongly about my husband's "wrong" decision?

We need to remember that your responsibility as a wife is to subject yourself to your husband. The man is responsible before God to make the decision that he deems best. "Wives, be subject to your husbands, as is fitting in the Lord" (Colossians 3:18).

It might further help to understand that when the husband is wrong, he usually already knows it. He is just looking for excuses. If a wife contends with her husband, then he normally becomes defensive. If however, she follows God's pattern, it allows the best situation to occur. In these cases, and I have personally experienced this numerous times, the quiet heart of the wife allows the Spirit of God to work in his heart. He will often come and ask her about these issues.

At times though, the husband is right and the wife is wrong. The wife needs to trust God through her husband's decisions. She needs to go by his judgment. God's command helps her to do the best thing possible even when she does not feel like it. Women are often confused by their feelings. They are situational creatures by design. Although she has much to contribute, she needs to learn how to bring that contribution to her family.

Some wives might wonder about abuse. "How did these women like Sarah do it?

We might be tempted to say things like, "Maybe Abraham wasn't as bad as my husband!" Unfortunately, we forget how bad Abraham was. Abraham responded in fear for his own life as he traveled to a foreign land. What did he do? He commanded his wife to tell them that she was only his sister. Abraham actually allowed these foreigners to take her into their harem (more than once!). Sarah faced confusing times when her husband Abraham made these moral compromises in his life which greatly impacted her. I wish I could say this was rare but it isn't.

So how does a wife endure this wrongful treatment?

We should first clarify God's will by asking, "Do you know any wives who have taken control of the home out of their husband's hands that have good marriages and families?" No. Every time a wife demands something or refuses her husband, she is hardened, and a wall is formed between them. There is no way to resolve this unless confession is made and that wall is taken down. If it isn't, then every aspect of their marriage will be tainted with evil, including their sexual lives.

There is no doubt that those who suffer under difficult situations need extra grace to endure. In some circumstances the financial stability of the whole home may be lost through the husband's foolish decisions. God permits such things to happen. He knows brokenness must come one way or the other if they are going to find true help. Obviously, God has a greater purpose. He wants to preserve and restore marriages. We need to accept such matters. Having a home is nice but it is not the most important thing in life. A wife must cry out to God when she sees her husband sailing them onto the rocks.

How does a wife cry out to God for help?

Crying out to God for help is one of the greatest themes across the pages of the Holy Scriptures. How many times does the scripture speak of help coming to those who cry out to God for help? Page after page record such situations. God specializes in helping people through crises. God created the oppression in Egypt that led to a greater good, that is, the Exodus. The Israelites were set free. God brought them under tremendous difficulties so that they could see His great saving hand. There are many reasons for the unhappy marriages we see today. But God specializes in restoring them. He restores our marriages by bringing us through difficult trials.

The vulnerability of people who receive God's love is similar to the vulnerability a wife has before an oppressive husband. The oppression suffered by God's people has similarities to that of a wife being oppressed by her husband. Perhaps careful observation of how God works with His people in desperate situations will help wives understand how He will help them in most difficult circumstances as they trust in Him.

God's love or power is not diminished when a wife is being emotionally or otherwise hurt by a senseless husband. Right now there are many such hurting wives.[25] God's love or power is not at all diminished when God allows His own people, His bride, to suffer from oppression. Right now I know of two Christian villages in one country that were invaded and taken possession of by a larger Moslem group. They lost everything including many lives. They are in a very desperate situation.

We assume God would not allow such things to occur, but He does for a time. Justice will come though. These times of oppression are allowed for special activities of God to occur. We are not trying to say God does the evil itself. God is not like that cruel husband. However, He does allow it to happen and works through its difficulties. God notices very carefully all His people who suffer and will take proper action and revenge. God is greater than evil by incorporating it into His glorious eternal plan. God at times tolerates suffering in His people.

---

[25] We should remember that some husbands are abused by their wives.

How long, O Lord, holy and true, wilt Thou refrain from judging and
avenging our blood on those who dwell on the earth?
And there was given to each of them a white robe; and they were told
that they should rest for a little while longer, until the number of their
fellow servants and their brethren
who were to be killed even as they had been, should be completed also.
(Revelation 6:9-11)

Actual examples of suffering from the Bible include Jesus and the early church.[26] Our immature concept of suffering is compounded by our love for ease and pleasure. Obedience sometimes has a high price tag. Wives need to be willing to endure suffering and shame in obedience to God.

Why do modern day women have an increased problem with submission?

The church and wives suffer a common ailment. When she becomes wealthy, she forgets how dependent she is. She begins to resent her position and wants more say in how things go. This is the heart that leads to an independent spirit and isolation. The lack of good prayer meetings to seek the Lord's direction is similar to the wife who makes decisions without first consulting her husband.

These problems increase when a wife has a career of her own. What are her temptations? Why are these difficult to handle?

The trouble is not just in the job that takes the wife away from her husband's service (e.g. make your own meal) but also results in interpersonal problems. There is no time for discussion. The wife forgets God's first calling to be a wife and instead follows her own 'more rewarding'

---

[26] Here are two passages: *"And Saul was in hearty agreement with putting him to death. And on that day a great persecution arose against the church in Jerusalem; and they were all scattered...." (Acts 8:12). "Therefore, we ourselves speak proudly of you among the churches of God for your perseverance and faith in the midst of all your persecutions and afflictions which you endure" (2 Thessalonians 1:4).*

independent lifestyle. She will not find fulfillment in that though. At times she may look for a relationship that fulfills her, usually outside her marriage leading to immorality. Wealth leads to a distorted perception of one's position, which causes great stress in the relationship.

Is it okay to discuss differences with a pastor or government workers?
The husband is the wife's authority. But there are other authorities that will at times observe inappropriate action by the husband and will try to correct it. God Himself does this. These are very difficult situations and cannot be completely discussed here. Let me make a few suggestions. Do not bring your husband's sin to the attention of a government authority, but let God do it in His own way, if indeed it needs to come to that.

A wife should, only if needed, carefully mention her general need to the elders or pastors so that they can pray for them. She should refrain from revealing specifics. If God so leads, let Him work through the elders by careful observation of him. The husband's sins might be against her, the children, or in some other context. A wife must refuse to stand as his accuser. She must be there to build him up when he is broken.

Allow God to handle the case. Cry out to Him. Pray that God would intervene and grant mercy to him. "Thou hast placed our iniquities before Thee, Our secret sins in the light of Thy presence" (Proverbs 90:8).

We realize that there is a great deal of differing advice about what one should do in such situations. Our general comments are made in light of a wife's chief calling and recognition of her authorities. We do not in any way imply that the husband is innocent or should be free from judgment. The wife, however, is called to support him rather than pull him down. She must be careful to avoid an adversarial position so that if by God's grace he is broken, their marriage can be restored.

Summary

Are you filled with zeal in serving your husband? Have you made those heart-rending decisions to no longer serve yourself but rather the living God?

When a wife has made these decisions, she becomes full of mysterious wonder. Her husband cannot but take notice. This does not mean he will tell the wife of his observations, but he will notice. Her selfless love is too ravishing not to pay close attention. He is absolutely blessed by her.

> "An excellent wife, who can find? For her worth is far above jewels" (Proverbs 31:10).

When the wife responds first to the Lord and then from the abundance of that relationship serves her husband, she is ready and able to meet her husband's spoken and unspoken requests. As she responds to the Lord Christ, so she responds to her husband.

Vulnerability and abuse are not times to give up on God's love. God's love and power never stop, even in the midst of persecution. God works through the crisis to display His great power. He enables His people to bear up under great pain and love when being hated or tested. This is the greatness of those who respond to His love in difficult circumstances. We are filled when we trust Him.

God's love is so awesome that it is sufficient for our every circumstance. We might be perplexed and sometimes hurt, but the Lord is carefully watching over us. When we can submit to His love in these situations, a great testimony goes forth. This is the response to His sacrificial love.

These statements should never be seen to excuse a man's irresponsible treatment of his wife or the world's oppression of a weak people. But just as a husband's love must endure a cold and foolish wife, so a wife must endure her foolish husband. A wife cannot say she will be responsive at certain times and hardened at other times depending on how her husband treats her. No. God's command to submit to her husband in everything shines as a beacon of light from His holy lighthouse in this dark world, even if it means facing difficult circumstances such as financial losses.[27]

FULFILLMENT OVERCOMES EMPTINESS

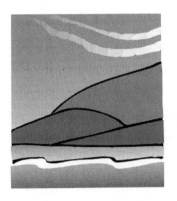

When we are responsive to God's love, our whole orientation toward life changes. When God's love is on our mind, we are thinking about others. If a wife is consumed with God's love, she will not insist or even ask her husband to follow her opinions.

Instead, being deeply satisfied in her heart and trusting herself to God, she submits to her husband. As she trusts God, her heart swells with God's love and overflows to those around her. Fullness of God's love chases away the emptiness.

The picture that comes to my mind is the ocean with its rising tide filling a once dry cove. As the water rises, it begins to fill all the empty spaces. There was rock and sand, but now as the water rises, swirling all around, every small cavity is filled. Then life, the crabs, the fish begin to fill the place that not long ago was barren and dry.

---

[27] Many wives have shared that they took over control of the house when they saw the husband start making foolish financial decisions. We should ask why did they start at that point? Is it perhaps that they love money more than God?

God's love seeks to fill our empty lives. The waves of God's love must push out the emptiness of self-pursuit to fill our lives with the much more glorious waves of pleasing and delighting others.

As trust increases, God's love begins to fill in the places that were before dry and barren.

A Wife's Action Plan

Right now, God is asking that every wife put away her selfishness. She needs to first respond to God's love by agreeing with Him. She needs to acknowledge how she has turned away from His loving plan and desire Him and His love now.

Tell Him that you want forgiveness for all of your insubmissive actions and poor attitudes. Confess how you didn't trust Him in those difficult circumstances. Through Jesus Christ you can find forgiveness for your sins, restoration, and a fresh start that never has an end. Acknowledge that He knows the best plan for your life and that you will trust Him to lead you to fulfill this plan, even when it includes submitting to a selfish husband.

Walking in humility,
Accepting my womanhood,

Gentle, quiet and kind.

Let me seek the welfare of others,
Allow me the privilege of faithfully serving my husband and family.

May my heart be content in fully pleasing my Lord.

A Wife's Prayer

Dear Lord, it is time for me to change. I have avoided my responsibilities. I have pursued my own desires and gone my own ways. All I have received is emptiness. I have not paid attention to you and your purposes. I have been too insistent on getting what I think I need. Here you have this great design for my life, and I have hardened myself to it.

I no longer want to be part of the problem, but rather with your love flowing through me, to be part of the solution. Lord, through Jesus Christ, please forgive me for my selfish ways and restore me to You. Forgive me for my insubmissive heart shown in both my attitudes and acts against my husband. I have let him down so much.

Grant me no greater passion than to respond fully and warmly to You and Your plans. Help me. My faith is so small. There will be times I will not understand Your ways, but I do desire them. Now may Your waves of love overflow and refresh my heart so that Your love in me may splash over into the lives of those around me.

Lord, I pray that you would help me be your faithful representative to my husband. I have made life difficult for him. I have not been sweet, lovely, and taken up every good desire of his. I have been selfish in my thinking; I have demanded my own time. I now affirm that I die to myself, O Lord. Let me serve You by faithfully serving him. Even if I might suffer, please help me to be faithful like Sarah. Someday, may it be said of me that I have the "imperishable quality of a gentle and quiet spirit, which is precious in the sight of God." Let me be one of the holy women of the present times, who in their hope in God, adorn themselves by being submissive to their own husbands. May you see my love for you through my faithful service to my husband. In Christ Jesus I pray, Amen.

Chapter #3 Study Questions

1. What is the second life principle?

2. Write out Ephesians 5:22.

3. What is God's design of marriage modeled after?

4. How does the church model a wife's response to her husband? (See Ephesians 5:24)

5. What is God's plan for the church? How is this accomplished?

6. What are two of the four truths that a wife needs to believe to rightly submit to her husband?

7. Who is trying to convince the wife that she should not submit to her husband? How does it occur?

8. What is the difference between a marriage contract and a marriage covenant?

9. Does being subject to another mean they are unimportant or invaluable? Why?

10. How does God look at human suffering? How should a wife look at potential suffering caused by a selfish husband?

11. Explain how fear cripples a relationship.

12. Show how love develops obedience and trust.

13. Explain how 1 Peter 3:3-4 paints a picture of a submissive wife.

14. Should a wife obey an evil husband? Why or why not? Are there any exceptions?

15. How should a wife respond to her husband when she doesn't see him loving her as he should?

16. How does wealth distort a woman's perception of submission to her husband?

Personal Reflection Questions

17. Have you been able to perceive the love of God?

18. Can you respond to His love?

19. Have you made a pledge to unwaveringly submit yourself to your husband? What might be holding you back?

#4 Oneness Forever: Life Principle 3

Couples are looking for that perfect marriage. Although we might not be able to find perfection here on earth, we can get pretty close by living out this third life principle of 'Oneness Forever.'

God's ways are amazingly simple yet intricate. Objects, for example, are made from different groupings of atoms. The water molecule is made from two hydrogen atoms and one oxygen atom. This seems so simple until we take a closer look at these atoms which seem to be a universe in themselves. A special powerful force keeps the different moving particles working together.

Marriage has a similar force. God has declared that the 'two become one flesh.' It seems easy and makes a lot of sense. But the more we think about it, we see that there are some very mysterious forces working behind marriage to keep it together.

Much like the atom, God's design for marriage is perfect. By some amazing feat one male and one female with different wills and bodies are willing to stay, live and work together throughout their lives. Even more remarkable is how through their lives develop new unique humans (we call them children) made from a composition of the original two. Each child is a beautiful expression of oneness.

The first two life principles hold a critical place in our marriages: Unconditional love and humble submission. They are principles that not only husbands and wives are asked to abide by but everyone all the time. Living out these truths is essential to a great marriage. We want to speak about the third life principle today.

This third life principle comes from Genesis 2:24 and is developed more fully in Ephesians 5, just as the other two life principles are. This is the mystery of marriage. "... And the two shall become one flesh. This mystery is great; but I am speaking with reference to Christ and the church" (Ephesians 5:31-32).

The fact is that the married couple is now 'one body' through the mighty declaration of God. We are called to recognize this oneness and affirm it. As we assert this unity in different practical ways, our marriages get stronger and stronger. And equally, as we choose not to live out this oneness, our marriages 'fall apart.' The less our lives comply with God's design, the greater the problems.

I remember once walking by a huge building that had collapsed while being built. Several people had even died. The constructors had not followed the design. In order to make money, they used thinner materials than were called for. From their point of view, everything was fine. They did not see the need for the original thickness called for by the designers. This huge public building was now a colossal mess. The same thing happens in marriages as we veer from the original design, even if we do not see immediate problems pop up.

Let's look more closely at this third life principle of "Oneness Forever." When we abide in oneness, a special security arises over our hearts that gives us freedom to rest, delight and dream. It is here in God's design that we find His protection as well as His harmony, love and joy for our marriages.

A) Life Principle #3: Oneness Forever

Marriage was meant to last. We all know the marriage vows, "as long as we both shall live." With so many different opinions being expressed today, we need to see what the Bible has to say about these matters. This concept is revealed in Genesis and repeated several times in the New Testament.

"For this cause a man shall leave his father and his mother, and shall cleave to His wife; and they shall become one flesh" (Genesis 2:24).

"For this cause a man shall leave his father and his mother, and shall cleave to His wife; and the two shall become one flesh." (Matthew 19:5)

We should note that Jesus' version varies just a bit. The scriptures first speak about a couple joining together. The man leaves the authority of his parents and becomes his own authority under God. This shift of family authority and structure indicates a long-term change. So does the way a man devotes himself to his new wife. The word "cleave" is very strong and has a sense of clinging, like vines to a tree trunk, or like when you accidentally super-glue your fingers together. Clinging demands concentrated focus, which precludes other behaviors or thoughts.

The element of permanency for marriage is even more clearly reflected in the last phrase where two people are joined into one new family unit. These verses are not just speaking about sexual intimacies. True, the sexual act, in an amazing way, reveals this oneness. The climax of the sexual act should unite the man and woman all at once in the heart, mind, and body. Oneness however goes beyond this brief and intense time of intimacy. The verse states that they become one flesh. A change occurs in their nature.

PHYSICAL ONENESS
SOUL ONENESS
SPIRITUAL ONENESS

This 'oneness' deeply touches the pledge of one's heart toward the other in an "as long as we both shall live" type of commitment. The oneness is created by a perfect blend of their two lives. The differing genders, responsibilities and physical features all assist in the creation of a masterpiece of oneness. There can hardly be found a more splendid truth stated by such simple words, "They shall become one flesh."

They are now one flesh, or unit; they are no longer two. There is intimate sharing of heart, soul and body. This glorious union reveals itself in the birth of 'their' child. One child shares equally from the husband and wife. We now know by a study of the cells that both the father and mother's oneness is incorporated together in every cell of the new baby. This is absolutely remarkable. If you want to affirm your marriage, have lots of children!

As we reflect upon this 'one flesh' concept, we notice something even more amazing. When something is one, it cannot be simply broken into normal functional pieces with new identities. The atom, which seems to be indivisible, really is comprised of different parts. The nucleus and electrons are mysteriously coupled together by awesome and mysterious forces. In order to break them apart, great energy is needed and the original elements are tremendously impacted. Just think what happens with the atom bomb. God has through His own judgment declared that the married couple is one. The male and female are promised to each other and become one for life. Only death removes this oneness.

No Division Allowed

Jesus further clarifies this. "Consequently they are no longer two, but one flesh. What therefore God has joined together, let no man separate" (Matthew 19:6).

God takes part in the wedding ceremony whether it took place in a church or not.[28] God has joined the couple together. The two have lost their separate identity. They have become one. After marriage, we can no longer find the original two. Yes, they are present and identifiable much like a nucleus and an electron, but to understand them one must understand how they are bonded together.[29] This is the reason divorce does not make sense and remarriage even less so (unless the original partner dies). Jesus simply says remarriage after divorce is the same as adultery.[30]

"And He said to them, "Whoever divorces his wife and marries another woman commits adultery against her" (Mark 10:11).

"A wife is bound as long as her husband lives; but if her husband is dead, she is free to be married to whom she wishes, only in the Lord" (1 Corinthians 7:39).

---

[28] God attends every marriage even without an invitation!

[29] World Book Encyclopedia (online) reports, "If a hydrogen atom were about 4 miles (6.4 kilometers) in diameter, its nucleus would be no bigger than a tennis ball. The rest of an atom outside the nucleus is mostly empty space. The electrons whirl through this space, completing billions of trips around the nucleus each millionth of a second."

[30] Some people argue that divorce is permissible if adultery is involved. They base this on a parallel passage in Matthew (Matthew 5:31-32) which adds, 'except for uncleanness.' The interpretation is equally split among scholars. We prefer the more consistent and clear interpretation that asserts that the Matthew passage alludes to a Deuteronomical law (Deuteronomy 24:1) granting Joseph permission to divorce Mary. If sexual purity cannot be established at marriage, then a man can divorce his wife. Only the Jewish people would understand this law and so it is only included in the Gospel of Matthew. This interpretation is further established by the disciples' response to Jesus, "Wow! If this is the case no one better get married" (Matthew 19:10 - my paraphrase).

A spouse cannot simply state that he or she is no longer pledged. A pledge is a pledge. Since the pledge is for life, then he must be faithful for life.[31] God has joined them together through His mysterious force. Although earthly courts permit divorce and nullification of marriage, the marriage continues to exist before God as long as both spouses live. [32]

In both cases there is treachery; a broken pledge of devotion and care.

Paul says the same thing about the church and her relationship with Christ. "Do you not know that your bodies are members of Christ? Shall I then take away the members of Christ and make them members of a harlot? May it never be!" (1 Corinthians 6:15)

Because of a prior spiritual commitment to Christ, we are one with Him. If we then give our devotion to another, this is spiritual adultery or idolatry. When a married person has sexual relations with another, or even entertains such thoughts, adultery occurs (Matthew 5:28).

Oneness most clearly shows itself in its indivisibility.

B) Marriage Alternatives?

Today there are any number of groups demanding alternative kinds of 'marriage.' The government and courts will decide in the end whether they will follow God's arrangement, which is so clearly given in Genesis, or their own depraved reasoning. As we have pointed out in another chapter, God made His point very clear in Genesis 2:24. He uses the

---

[31] We must wonder whether those who pledge "as long as we love each other" is really a marriage after all or is it an excuse for fornication?

[32] The Roman Catholic church and others have completely confused this by creating 'annulments' or statements that the marriage never existed. This is a complete sham and ought to be immediately done away with.

male and female words for husband and wife. The male leaves his parents and cleaves to the female. There is no room for what people call homosexual 'marriages.'[33]

This is obvious in a physical or natural realm, but evil men are so intent on fulfilling their lusts, they no longer want to even accept the obvious lessons from nature, let alone from God's Word. Two males do not make one. Neither do two females. God did not state that they become one because they are still two. Even our little children know one male plus one male equals two males.

The female was specially designed to complement the male. If God wanted another male to keep Adam company. He would have made another man. Instead He went out of His way to create an entirely new gender that fully complemented man in marriage. From this union they bear the fruit of children.

We are not saying that man or woman cannot live fulfilling lives as singles. They can. 1 Corinthians 7 clearly prescribes this possibility when a man or woman gains their fullness from closeness to God and bears the fruit of good works (rather than children). The apostle says, "But I want you to be free from concern. One who is unmarried is concerned about the things of the Lord, how he may please the Lord" (1 Corinthians 7:32).

Another increasingly popular lifestyle is not to get married at all but still obtain marital privileges. Many young and old people alike no longer want to enter marriage. They have at some point in the past been scarred. They no longer have dreams of oneness. Their bubbles of hope have been popped. This generation is afraid of commitment because they have seen the terrible way marriages often end up. They no longer believe that marriage can be good.

---

[33] The word for female simply has one sound added to the word for male.

A society cannot easily turn back. Blatant immorality and adultery are signs of a degenerate generation. The solution is first for Christian couples to live out their one-

ness and then challenge others to live out their vows. God has brought revival to us before and changed the culture in an instant, but God's people first need to repent and seek His face.

Living together outside of marriage is not marriage; it is fornication. The two are not living under the promise of marriage. They are not 'one flesh' but two who are harming each other for their own selfish purposes.

Marriage is designed to last as long as both husband and wife live on earth. Marriage provides us with the most beautiful picture of continuity and development one could find on earth. Marriage ends as a spouse dies, but in its temporariness it forms a beautiful analogy of a greater eternal relationship between God and His people (c.f. Revelation 21:2).

The truth of this oneness has great ramifications for our marriage. To the degree that we accept by faith this oneness, we will live by its implicit truths. This will in turn lead to a great marriage. Without faith in this oneness, our marriages will suffer as we adopt one of the world's convenient ways of explaining marriage. There is no middle path. To avoid living by the principles of oneness is to disaffirm them. Good marriages always strengthen that affirmation by living out that oneness.

C) A Strong Marriage Foundation

Foundations are what we build structures upon. A marriage has certain foundational truths. If the foundation is not solid, then, no matter how well something is built on top of that foundation, it will suffer. This is the problem with earthquakes. Earthquakes shake foundations. They test those foundations for their strength. The seams or weaknesses in land mass are called faults. It is at these huge faults that the greatest damage occurs. Anything built on those faults crumbles. A spirit of oneness obliterates these seams while a spirit of divorce amplifies them.

Today many couples get married thinking that divorce is a possibility. Some are quite open about it. "If it doesn't work out, then we will get a divorce." Divorce looks like an easy solution. A couple might not openly acknowledge this, but if the potentiality of divorce remains in the mind, it becomes a weakness that the evil one will later use to further trouble their marriage. Marriages will be shaken with all sorts of life challenges.

One reason God hates divorce is because it counters the beautiful picture of oneness and induces many devastating consequences. Even secular research clearly outlines the pain, loneliness and wretchedness of divorce. Marriage fidelity liberates us to enjoy God's goodness rather than being imprisoned in what some want us to believe is an ancient tradition, the pass.

Another dangerous tendency in wealthy societies is for the husband and wife to associate material blessings with a good marriage. Excitement over, a new furniture, a new home or even a new baby might disguise marital problems for a while, but they will eventually rise up. The couple might have made vows of marrying for life, but when troubling times come, they begin to think of separation and divorce as real possibilities.

When troubles between a married couple grow, temptations step in to lure the commitment of spouses away from each other. The husband imagines what it would be like with another woman. The wife tries to think through her financial situation to see if she can support herself. These very thoughts shake the foundation of the marriage.

How a person responds to these thoughts reveals their commitment to the oneness in their marriage. Every marriage faces challenges. Our responses to these challenges depend on what we really believe. In the end, a couple may show that they do not really believe that they are one for life. This is seen by their contemplation of other options in troubling times.

Be careful. I do not want to imply that the mere thought of another 'better life' reveals what we believe. Satan often interjects thoughts into our minds. We know what we believe by what we decide. Our choices should reject these unbiblical thoughts and affirm that oneness. Don't let these temptations lure you to think and decide otherwise. Examples of this will be provided later in this chapter.

Some couples are deeply shocked when these thoughts of divorce are first brought up. Their dreams are broken; they are devastated. They think it is all over. This is not true.

Although it may seem impossible for a marriage to turn around, it can. The couple can sort things out by focusing on the truth of their oneness. They need to set their hearts upon living by their marriage vows. This is the way it is for every married couple. When we decide to live by the fact of oneness, then the marriage can hold together. Other matters become secondary. We make changes to reinforce the concept of oneness.

If, however, either spouse is willing to accept the temptation to live apart from God's binding truth and choose a path separate from their spouse, then the couple will experience great turmoil. We will discuss in a later chapter what special steps can be taken when a spouse begins to talk about leaving, or in fact does leave.

The Ranch

This 'oneness' life principle might still sound rather vague. It is hard to comprehend! Let's try to get a better handle on its meaning.

When a person walks around his thousand-acre ranch encircled by a fence, he will rarely run into the fence. He can walk and walk and never meet up with the defining edge of his property. Good marriages are similar. The husband might work in the city, fly to visit his father, or take a bus back home all in the confines of marital oneness. The husband and wife are one even though they are separate.

However, if an attractive young lady walks alluringly by the husband, then that fence will suddenly appear. He knows he needs to delight only in the wife of his youth. He turns his mind and eyes away from her. What is he doing? He is affirming the oneness of his marriage. He accepts the help of the fence. The fence reminds him of this oneness. He then affirms the pledge to desire only his wife. He stays within the fence.

The wife might be reading a romance novel. She starts identifying herself with the woman in the story and begins to want such a romantic

man as portrayed in the story. Her husband is completely dull! The fence arises. She is starting to covet someone else's man (even though in this case he might be imaginary). She remembers her pledge to support and love her unromantic (up to now – always keep hoping) husband. She refuses to entertain that anyone else could be better for her than who the spouse she now has.

She follows through her commitment by instantly returning the book to the library. She furthermore thanks the Lord for her husband and in her heart affirms her pledge to him alone. Did you see the pattern? She identifies what threatens that oneness, rejects it, and practically affirms that oneness.

We have only started touching upon this mighty life principle of oneness. As with the other life principles, they all have to do with living out our Christian life. Before proceeding any further, we would like to explain this life principle in its spiritual context. Perhaps this will enable us to better understand how this oneness principle applies to our own marriages.

D) The Spiritual Analogy

This oneness principle is written about in many scriptural passages including the Old Testament. This is because salvation is built upon the concept of the covenant between God and man. We will concentrate on the New Testament teaching. The New Testament teaches us the basic truth that Christians are part of a covenant with God through Christ. They are in Christ and one with Christ because they are joined to Christ.

This is most clearly seen by the phrase "in Christ" repeated through the Bible. It is used 88 times! The phrase 'in Christ' or 'in Him' is used eleven times just in the first chapter of Ephesians. Let us look at just three examples.[34]

> *"Blessed be the God and Father of our Lord Jesus Christ, who has blessed us with every spiritual blessing in the heavenly places in Christ" (Ephesians 1:3).*
>
> *"Just as He chose us in Him before the foundation of the world, that we should be holy and blameless before Him. In love" (Ephesians 1:4).*

---

[34] Ephesians 1:1,3,4,7,9,10,12,13,20.

"In Him we have redemption through His blood, the forgiveness of our trespasses, according to the riches of His grace" (Ephesians 1:7).

We are special because we are in Christ. It is our position in Christ that joined us to God's love and promises. We are one in Christ. This is the teaching of baptism and is clearly taught in Romans.

"Or do you not know that all of us who have been baptized into Christ Jesus have been baptized into His death? Therefore we have been buried with Him through baptism into death, in order that as Christ was raised from the dead through the glory of the Father, so we too might walk in newness of life. For if we have become united with Him in the likeness of His death, certainly we shall be also in the likeness of His resurrection, knowing this, that our old self was crucified with Him, that our body of sin might be done away with, that we should no longer be slaves to sin; for he who has died is freed from sin. Now if we have died with Christ, we believe that we shall also live with Him" (Romans 6:3-8).

Baptism is a physical ceremony that displays our oneness with Christ. This is like the bride walking up the center aisle to be wed. She leaves her family to join the bridegroom in making a new family. She loses her old identity (last name) and becomes part of a new identity by adopting his last name.[35] Together they begin a new life.

Struggles will arise that will test our allegiance to Christ. However, we must obey our Lord and disregard our decisions associated with our old identity. This works out practically in a marriage when the husband requests one thing of the wife, but she is pressured by her mother to do something to the contrary, perhaps regarding child discipline. She must live out her oneness with her husband and do as he requests. Notice how this thought was developed in Romans 6:11 with reference to Christ and the church.

---

[35] We realize this reflects the practice only in certain countries. Be that as it may, it fully reflects what happens when a woman marries a man. She becomes his.

> "Even so consider yourselves to be dead to sin, but alive to God in Christ Jesus" (Romans 6:11).

We can see this truth or life principle of oneness worked out in all sorts of passages. Below is Paul's advice to the Philippians.

> *"Only conduct yourselves in a manner worthy of the gospel of Christ; so that whether I come and see you or remain absent, I may hear of you that you are standing firm in one spirit, with one mind striving together for the faith of the gospel; in no way alarmed by your opponents--which is a sign of destruction for them, but of salvation for you, and that too, from God" (Philippians 1:27-28).*

How do they stand firm against the enemy that threatens their faith in Christ? It is through their commitment to Christ. "Stand firm in one spirit, with one mind." Whenever we stand firm in our covenant commitment, the enemy is exposed for what he is – an adulterer trying to lure us away.

A Unique Angle

Before we move on, we want to look at one more passage that differs from the others. Romans 7:2-4 marvelously links together these three teachings: the marriage covenant, the Christian covenant and oneness. Paul uses the concept of Old Testament law to understand the nature of a covenant like the marriage covenant.

> *"For the married woman is bound by law to her husband while he is living; but if her husband dies, she is released from the law concerning the husband. So then if, while her husband is living, she is joined to another man, she shall be called an adulteress; but if her husband dies, she is free from the law, so that she is not an adulteress, though she is joined to another man. Therefore, my brethren, you also were made to die to the Law through the body of Christ, that you might be joined to another, to Him who was raised from the dead, that we might bear fruit for God" (Romans 7:2-4).*

The only way a marriage is dissolved is through death. Marriages on earth last only as long as both partners live. Divorce is man's idea to free a couple from their commitment, but it does not free them from the commitment that was made before God. God has united them, whether they acknowledge it or not. The same is true regarding our salvation. We died to our old identity and self through faith in Christ and are united in Christ's new purpose. And just as in marriage there is fruit from the union (children being the most prominent), so there is fruit from our union in Christ (see John 15:5).

The strength of a marriage, or of a Christian, similarly depends on how much they clearly identify with their oneness. In the spiritual realm, Satan wants us to rock our foundation by shaking our faith. He does this by causing us to question whether or not we are really saved. Satan does this in our marriage too, by tempting us to think we have options other than staying married. Let's look at how Satan whittles away at the foundations of marriage in our modern society.

E) Modern Marriage and its Temptations

We would love to say that the church is faithfully proclaiming God's teaching on marriage. Unfortunately, this is not so. There are some churches staying faithful to God's Word. Overall, however, the church is not only permitting divorce, but encourages divorcees to think of themselves as 'singles.' They sponsor groups to help them find another partner. God hates this spirit of divorce and remarriage because it goes against this principle of oneness.

> "For I hate divorce," says the LORD, the God of Israel, "and him who covers his garment with wrong," says the LORD of hosts. "So take heed to your spirit, that you do not deal treacherously" (Malachi 2:16).

The Lord hates divorce because it breaks the basic life principle of one flesh. A divorcee has dealt treacherously with their marriage partner. Formerly, only the man would initiate divorce but now with more wealth, the woman also feels free to initiate divorce. God's heart is broken over this. What is happening in the physical realm is also happening in the spiritual realm. People are leaving Christ. They are rejecting their obedient tie to the Lord. The tie between marriage and salvation is much closer than many of us suspect.[36]

This is also apparent by the way adultery sullies the marriage as well as one's spiritual life. The spirit of adultery is all around us. I personally would be bound by this sin if it wasn't for the grace of God. Let us look at how oneness is threatened by pornography.

(1) Pornography, sensual viewing and reading

Some people consider pornography a needed and normal diversion for boys and men. I have even heard of Christian parents who think they are teaching their sons about marriage through exposing them to pornography. Pornography has nothing to do with marriage! These parents are not introducing them to marriage but to adultery.

If they want to teach about oneness, then parents must keep their children from pornography and give them a vision of delighting themselves only in the one woman of their future. We are grieved by what is happening all around us. Jesus stated in clear words that the heart of pornography is adultery. Read Matthew 5:28 below.

---

[36] See the emphasized words in this passage. Marriage problems reveal spiritual problems, *"But realize this, that in the last days difficult times will come. For men will be lovers of self, lovers of money, boastful, arrogant, revilers, disobedient to parents, ungrateful, unholy, unloving, irreconcilable, malicious gossips, without self-control, brutal, haters of good, treacherous, reckless, conceited, lovers of pleasure rather than lovers of God"* (2 Timothy 3:1-4).

"But I say to you, that everyone who looks on a woman to lust for her has committed adultery with her already in his heart"

In other words, the spouse that has set his or her eyes on another with lust has denied the fact of their oneness. They have allowed their own self-indulgent desires to rule over their loyalty to their spouse. They are one but no longer embrace that truth. They are instead fostering false oneness with another.

Women are susceptible to the same temptation. An increasing number of women use pornography. They are looking for substitute relationships. By tolerating pornography, sensual movies, or novels, they are developing a spirit of treachery. They are turning their back on their vow to their spouse. This happens because they no longer place their confidence in the truth that God's way is best. The cure for those caught in the web of pornography is to confess the impurity of their hearts to God and their spouses.[37] Then they must renew the pledge to serve only the Lord by being faithful to their spouse. Let's look at it in a positive way.

Oneness tells me that God has given me a mighty good thing in a wife. The scriptures state, "He who finds a wife finds a good thing, and obtains favor from the LORD" (Proverbs 18:22).

We must be content with our spouse. As we purpose to delight only in our spouse, we reaffirm our oneness with him or her. The more we delight in our spouse, the bigger the 'ranch' gets. We sense more and

---

[37] I was greatly disturbed to hear a Christian counselor recommend that the husband not tell his wife of his sin of pornography in order to "spare" her. Although we appreciate that he was trying to be sensitive to the wife, it is ungodly advice. What kind of marriage does he want? If they want a great marriage, then they need to build from the foundation of oneness, which will not tolerate any deceit or darkness. As long as the man hides such destructive things from his wife, there can be no healing. He is covering sin and will not prosper. He needs to confess and seek forgiveness for these sins from her.

more freedom. As Paul says in Timothy, "the law is only for the lawless."[38] When we do not compromise our heart's pledge, then the law, i.e. the fence, is not thought of. The many surrounding temptations become less and less alluring. Why? We find joy in the fulfillment of God's promises.

We understand that some have given up hope. They call themselves addicted. The pull of chemical highs hiding behind sexual lusts can be very strong. Counselors tell them they are 'wounded' from the past. However, we must understand that when a husband or wife allows himself or herself to desire another, he or she is committing treachery. They are breaking their pledge. Repentance does not mean just trying to stop watching porn on the web.

The root of the problem must be exposed. They have been living by 'twoness' rather than oneness. They live as if they can make decisions apart from the other. Such actions reveal one's doubt that God's way is best and are in that way a rebellion against God's truth. Whenever one spurns God's truth, he will be burned by his rejection of it.

In fact, when we get a clear perspective of the life principle of oneness, we will see that bad marriages are filled with behavior that denies oneness. They allow themselves to make decisions that go against the oneness of marriage. Pornography is only one example. Let's think about another area: arguments.

(2) Fighting and Arguing

Jesus once said that it is crazy to think of someone that would fight with himself[39], but this is exactly what happens when spouses argue. When-

---

[38] *"Realizing the fact that law is not made for a righteous man, but for those who are lawless and rebellious, for the ungodly and sinners, for the unholy and profane, for those who kill their fathers or mothers, for murderers" (1 Timothy 1:9).*

[39] *"And if Satan casts out Satan, he is divided against himself; how then shall his kingdom stand?" (Matthew 12:26)*

ever a husband or wife opposes the other, he or she is like a malicious cell that has gone wild and is bent on destroying itself. They are countering the oneness life principle. They need to work together rather than oppose each other.

This might sound rather ideal, but this is where Jesus' command to love one another gets very practical. Are we not to strive to love one another? I have heard too many Christians state that arguments are normal, good and even needed. These so-called counselors are not doing anybody any good. Arguments and fights are not normal though they are common. Once we accept them as normal, then this sets the standard. Instead, we need to hold onto God's standard and repent from our argumentative spirits.

Spouses do have differences of opinion. We do have disagreements, but when we start criticizing or using words that intentionally hurt or belittle, we have surely forgotten the life principle of oneness. This truth is for all Christians. The apostle summarizes the approach we should take toward one another.

"And so, as those who have been chosen of God, holy and beloved, put on a heart of compassion, kindness, humility, gentleness and patience; bearing with one another, and forgiving each other, whoever has a complaint against anyone; just as the Lord forgave you, so also should you. And beyond all these things put on love, which is the perfect bond of unity" (Colossians 3:12-14).

There are more important things than expressing, insisting on, or enforcing one's own desires and thoughts. When a couple esteems God's will and ways, the way we do something is just as important as what we do. The couple must be willing to exercise humility and patience to accomplish the Lord's purpose. We acknowledge that due to our sinful self, we do fall from this standard whether it be in our marriage or in a church business meeting.

When the standard is high, as God has set it, we are able to repent, be restored and get back to where God wants us to be. Without such expectations, bitterness remains lodged in our hearts and slowly destroys all sense of oneness.

F) Affirmations of Oneness

Let's think of some positive ways to affirm oneness. Perhaps you already are doing many of them.

1. Commit yourself to never mention or even entertain the thought of divorce or separation of any kind as a possible way out.

2. Spend time together. Have a 'date' once a week.

3. Completely forgive the other for their sins. Don't harbor bitterness. "Love covers a multitude of sins."

4. Express affection and desire for each other beyond the bedroom.

5. Talk together about issues, dreams, children and other needs.

6. Think through and discuss how you complement each other.

7. Preserve your sexual intimacies as the scripture dictates (1 Corinthians 7:5).

8. Refuse to argue with each other. Acknowledge differences but then start to prayerfully discuss the issues.

9. Pray together regularly. (More than at meal time!)

10. Study God's Word together.

11. Develop a family vision. (How does God want you as a family to minister in this world?)

Oneness Forever

Steps of Affirmation

How can we climb these steps of affirmation? Let me share from my own journey. The principle behind all of these steps centers around clearly devoting myself to loving and delighting in my wife Linda. By doing this, she also develops an increasing love and joy. Temptations more easily stay away. Here are some basic ways I express that oneness beyond what was said above.

- Determine to only love my wife.
- Affirm my love for my wife by fighting off temptation.
- Trust God's timing to fulfill my own desires and needs. This helps guard me from frustration.
- Refuse to get bitter. She might be deluded by her feelings. She needs my kindness right now. I will wait for this mood to pass.
- Quickly apologize for my wrongs. I want us to work together.
- Remember that God's best way is to work through both of us. I need her!
- Remember that unless I have peace with her, God will not answer my prayers.[40]
- The greatest joys come through being in harmony with her. The worse times are when we are acting contrary to each other.

In future discussions, we hope to turn to more specific issues. We must master answers to these questions in order to preserve our oneness.

❖ How do you handle a situation where an argument is erupting?

❖ What if only one spouse is focusing on oneness?

❖ How can I handle his stinging words?

❖ Our marriage is built on bitterness? How do I get rid of it?

---

[40] *"You husbands likewise, live with your wives in an understanding way, as with a weaker vessel, since she is a woman; and grant her honor as a fellow heir of the grace of life, so that your prayers may not be hindered" (1 Peter 3:7).*

❖ I worry over whether my husband really loves me. What do I do?

❖ What do we do when we differ on an important issue?

Summary

The third life principle of oneness creates harmony. A couple does not simply become two at some point in life. Marriage is secured for a lifetime. From this security of love and commitment, love, joy and peace easily grow.

I am not competing with my spouse. No contests are allowed except to love each other more. We work together to get God's work done. Instead of figuring out ways to meet my own needs, I look for strategic places I can make sacrifices so I can demonstrate my commitment to oneness. My heart has become truly joyful and satisfied. Our foundation of oneness goes deeper and deeper, eliminating cracks and fissures that were not even seen before.

"And they lived happily ever after." This truth is symbolized and taught through a loyal and lifelong marriage. Like a Christian who has learned the glorious spiritual truths of identification with Christ, so marriage is like a storehouse of joy and love. We only need to stay focused on affirming the commitment to oneness. We make a commitment, and we stick to it. For life.

Appendix:

1) Our Commitment

I pledge to be a one-woman man. I have made my choice. I am married. No matter what problems I face, I trust the Lord to fulfill my life through my wife. I reject the temptations around me. I say a permanent "no" to my lusts. I have been called by God to unconditionally love my wife. She will be the one I delight in. She is the one that God in His time will use to fulfill my needs.

There might be difficult times, misunderstandings, or even outright rejection. I stand firm in my love for her. I trust God to enable me to keep my commitment. She will be the one I share my heart and vision with. She will be the one I cry with. I pledge to keep working on those rough spots that keep my wife from trusting my full devotion to her. At the same time I pledge to God that I will live only for Him and in that devotion give my heart to my wife.

2) Our Prayer

Dear Heavenly Father, I never realized how much I have made a mess of our marriage until now. Now I understand what 'oneness' means. Although you have pronounced us one, I have been living as two. I have argued and even fought with my spouse. O Lord, do forgive me and thoroughly cleanse me by your blood.

From this day forth I am fully devoting myself to my spouse. I want that devotion and love to be whole and not in any way fragmented, divided or broken. From now on, I will draw on your wisdom and advice to solve difficulties or problems in my marriage. Only let me build now on oneness rather than self.

Whether in bed, walking to the store, or in the car together, allow the glory and beauty of oneness to touch our hearts with Your peace, harmony, love and joy. These are what you promise and now I ask you for them. In Christ's Name I pray, Amen.

"Put me like a seal over your heart, like a seal on your arm.

For love is as strong as death, jealousy is as severe as Sheol;

Its flashes are flashes of fire, the very flame of the LORD.

Many waters cannot quench love, nor will rivers overflow it;

If a man were to give all the riches of his house for love,

It would be utterly despised"

(Song of Solomon 8:6-7).

Chapter #4 Study Questions

1. What is the third life principle?

2. How does an atom demonstrate this oneness?

3. What scripture is this principle built upon? Say it or write it down.

4. What makes a good or bad marriage?

5. Why is divorce or annulment not acceptable?

6. Why is remarriage to divorced people considered adultery?

7. Explain the concept of the 'ranch.'

8. List two ways this oneness concept is seen in the redemptive message of the New Testament.

9. Explain how pornography and other sensual perusing destroys a couple's oneness.

10. Explain how arguments and fights deny a couple's oneness.

11. List three ways to positively affirm your oneness with your spouse.

Personal Reflections

1. Have you affirmed your desire for oneness to your spouse?

2. Have you gained the self-control necessary to be content with only your spouse through your whole life?

3. Think through your own life and list three ways you have recently
   affirmed the oneness of your marriage in a practical sense.

Section #2: Forgiveness

Chapters #5-7

Restoring Broken Marriages

Building a
Great Marriage

#5 Understanding and Overcoming Conflict

Marital Conflict Resolution: Part 1

Is it possible to bring God's peace to your home? To your marriage? We believe so! One of the fruit of the Holy Spirit is peace (Galatians 5:22). In this chapter we will show you how a couple can turn an argumentative home into a home of harmony and love.

God's design really does work. We simply go back to what God has given to us and take hold of it: oneness. Harmony in the marriage relationship stems from the oneness God has granted a couple.

Many questions linger in our minds about how to practically reach that point of harmony. We will address these issues in two ways. First, by better increasing our understanding on how quarrels develop. Why do those who love each other fight or argue? After understanding the source of conflict, we will provide positive steps we can take to bring God's harmony to our hearts and home.

A) Understanding Marital Conflict (James 4:1-3)

Most of you could tell me the last two or three things you argued about. They are still on your mind because they have hurt you. In many cases they are still unresolved. This is the way it is with hostilities. One person might win that conflict. But because the other person lives next to you, they have lots of resources to make life difficult for the winner. No one really wins.

One might win the battle but not the war. These troubles go deeper than the actual issue that a couple might argue over. Fortunately, God has provided some very clear words about quarrels.

The word for argument is not frequently used in the scripture. Scripture uses the word largely to mean 'logical reasoning.' Most of our conflicts are anything but logical reasons presented back and forth – though we deeply believe that we are in the right. The problem is greatly aggravated when one is willing to verbally or perhaps physically, hurt his or her spouse to cause the spouse to win the fight. What have they really won?

James 4:1-3 like old time surgery, opens before us the heart of quarrels and conflicts. Look carefully at these words.

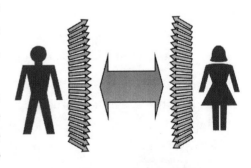

"What is the source of quarrels and conflicts among you? Is not the source your pleasures that wage war in your members?
You lust and do not have; so you commit murder. And you are envious and cannot obtain; so you fight and quarrel. You do not have because you do not

ask. You ask and do not receive, because you ask with wrong motives, so that you may spend it on your pleasures" (James 4:1-3).

Before drawing some general observations regarding conflicts, let us first look at two key Greek words used here: quarrels and conflicts. They are used twice, first in noun form and then in verb form (though in reverse order). Quarrel refers to the larger scale conflict: the war itself. Conflict is the word for battle. One literally could translate it 'source of wars and battles among you?'

Quarrels then refer to long-standing unresolved war along with all of the tensions and underlying issues at stake. Conflict on the other hand refers to individual battles or

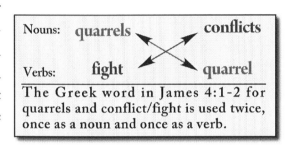

Nouns: **quarrels**   **conflicts**

Verbs: **fight**   **quarrel**

The Greek word in James 4:1-2 for quarrels and conflict/fight is used twice, once as a noun and once as a verb.

fights. Most couples are more aware of the conflicts than the long-standing 'war.' They pay more attention to the wounds from the last battle than to the real reason for marital infighting.

Uncontrolled anger is a real problem in marriage and exacerbates these fights. Anger is a tool that helps one perform a job more quickly. Unfortunately, in this case it is the destruction of one's spouse. Anger, similar to the spirit of conflict, destroys marriages because it acts contrary to the spirit of oneness. (Check here for more resources on handling anger).

If you solve a conflict, will you solve the quarrel (i.e. the war)? No. We need to go deeper, much deeper like James does. It is rather amusing to think that nobody likes these spats, including God, but we still participate in them! Now let us draw some observations from the words he has penned under God's direction so that we can rightly understand how to solve our conflicts.

Six observations on marriage quarrels

Each starts off by providing biblical evidence for the following conclusion.

1) Quarrels require cooperation. Two are needed!

Both the Greek words James uses have the sense of two sides: war and battle. Notice the word 'members' is also used. This refers to limbs of a body. There is fighting within.

We tend to fault our spouses for our problems, but we should be humble enough to accept that marital arguments require both the husband and wife. Great improvement comes when I refuse to see my spouse as the enemy.

2) Quarrelers are motivated to please themselves.

The word for pleasure (*hedone*) in James 4:1 is the root word for 'hedonism,' which is the popular philosophy of living to please oneself, me before others.

A couple needs to carefully examine what their life goals are. Without careful thought, the world's thoughts will influence their attitudes and decision-making process. Jesus said to prefer others above oneself.

3) The actual pursuit to fulfill one's desires causes conflict.

James 4:2 says that they "cannot obtain; so you fight and quarrel." They are driven so much by their desires that they are willing to cause trouble in the lives of others to get what they want. This is the opposite of love. There is no thought of God; they are self-driven.

Sometimes spouses get a plan in their mind that they suspect will not be accepted by the spouse. He or she might get sneaky and carry it out despite possible objections. At other times they will manipulate the other into an agreement. Remember Delilah's sweet words?

4) Quarrelers lack self-restraint and self-control.

They obviously have no self-control or at least do not want to exercise it. "...So you commit murder. ... so you fight and quarrel." They do wrong to the other.

"That is the way he is." Actually we all have a sin nature. The point is some spouses will repent and turn to God for His Spirit to help them and their marriage. Others will not. They will justify their actions. We all are responsible for our deeds.

5) Quarrelers do not seek God's way.

James 4:2 says, 'You do not ask.' They do not have a mind to seek what God wants or even to think how He might provide for them. Their prayers are manipulative, much like witchcraft. They are willing to go around God to get their wishes.

Some husbands and wives are not use to seeking help from God. They know how to get what they want – they have been doing it for years. They are willing to act mean, savage, sweet or even threaten their spouse just to get their own way.

6) Quarrelers lack a perspective of peace or oneness.

They accept the assumption that to gratify oneself is more important than the general welfare of the whole. In this case the church is referred to, but the same things happen in a marriage. The harmony (oneness) of a marriage is not prioritized.

If a couple lives without a commitment to oneness, then they will compete against each other. Peace will be substituted for disharmony until they change their commitment and live according to their oneness.

A Perspective on Wealth

When both couples are working, some of their quarrels will be eliminated. Some work just to avoid arguments. This reduction in conflicts can result from just being isolated from each other, but James points out that there is more to the important issue of money.

When the purse strings are tight, each spouse needs to give up more. The couple makes decisions and sacrifices together for a greater purpose that builds up a marriage. When each has their own job, they tend to buy what he or she wants. Their individual wants are satisfied. There is no team spirit. The other spouse doesn't have much say about it. James says conflicts begin when they do not get what they want.

Each person has a selfish tendency that will war against a good marriage. If we give into this independent self-seeking spirit, then we will become more argumentative, arrogant and plain selfish.

Just because a couple's wealth protects them from arguing over 'things', this does not mean they a good marriage. They just do not realize how they are living in the spirit of divorce. They have made separate lives for themselves. The tempter can easily cause them to stumble because of the way they live (or should we say 'do not live') out their marriage. Some use Proverbs 31 to justify working outside the home. By closely examining this passage, we will discover that the wife focused upon meeting the needs of her husband and home. She worked diligently to fulfill her duties. One can easily see where her heart was. She had a spirit of service. There was no spirit of 'twoness' in that marriage.

Our recommendation is for a wealthy couple to focus on special projects that they work on together, perhaps those to help those in need. This will help them focus on a common purpose and heart. Work together. Love together. This will affirm the foundation of oneness needed for a great marriage. (This advice is also good for those who feel their marriages are rather dull at the moment).

Summary

We can spend all our time discussing this passage in James and not learn how to solve marital conflict. But before we move on, let us summarize this discussion on conflict by recognizing that the real source of conflict is our own hearts. We allow ourselves to prioritize our own preferences over the well-being of the whole, in this case, our spouse and marriage. This is true in a church or in a marriage. The reason we become so aggressive in meeting our own needs is because of our selfish nature. We can even become pushy or selfish which always results in impolite and unkind behavior. Deep down in our heart, our goal is to please ourselves.

Some people have mastered the use of fear, anger, self-pity, worry, or silence as a means to get what they want. They regularly approach a situation in a certain manner to get what they 'need'.[41] God instead wants us to live by faith and obedience. Faith is the necessary trust in God to help you accomplish what He is asking you to do in a way pleasing to the Lord.

Now frankly if you are non-Christian, you need to come to know Jesus. Jesus not only takes our sins away but also gives us a new nature built on love. Everyone's old nature runs on the same fuel of selfishness. There are many who profess to be Christians just because they raised their hand as a child. That might shape where you go to church on Sunday, but it doesn't change your heart. You need to repent from your selfish person, seek cleansing in Christ's blood by believing in Jesus and start living out Christ's Spirit of love that now generates your new life. If you don't want to live God's way of love, then you need to be saved. Your lusts are ruling you and will take you into eternal judgment.

If you are a genuine Christian and still struggle greatly with these issues, we can be confident that God is able to and desires to help us out

---

[41] In many cases these are things we have learned from the homes we grew up in.

of our difficulties faster than we ever thought possible. We have the power to live a godly life in Christ by living out the fruit of the Spirit. Of course, we can also by choice or deception fall to living by our old nature. Think of a car with two gears.

When you put the car in one gear, it will always go forward. But if you put it in the other gear called reverse, it will always lead you backwards. What direction do you want to go in your marriage? You will either choose to live by the Spirit or the old selfish nature. By living by God's Spirit, you will serve Him and others. By living by the flesh, you will serve those old desires of yours.[42]

Steps to Bring Relief from Past Conflict

If your marriage has had these fights and quarrels, then you have been missing out on God's great design of marriage. Though you will have disagreements, you need to stop thinking that argumentation is the way to resolve those conflicts. Here are a few steps to help you out of your quagmire.

+ Identify these pleasures or desires of yours. What is it that has been driving you into conflict?

+ Repent from seeking your own desires rather than God's will. Focus on your own shortcomings rather than those of your spouse.

+ Patch up 'war' scars. When you have hurt others, then apologize, confess your wrong and ask for forgiveness. Confess your sins before God and your spouse. Do not leave past sins hidden away. They will keep presenting themselves as a barrier between you and your spouse until resolved.

+ Commit to living out God's oneness principle regardless of the consequences. You as a Christian are to serve God. What you want or think you need is secondary.

---

[42] This is Joshua's point in Joshua 24:19-25.

+ Trust God for the issues at stake. Trust Him for the way to work through these issues. Become convinced that His way is always better than your own. Do what He wants. Talk without action is empty. (More on this is coming.)

We have learned a lot about conflict. We have even begun to identify some real issues that lie beneath the arguments that couples have. We must resist trying to first solve the conflicts before understanding and dealing with why there is war in the first place. Some people are glad to win this or that battle but have never asked why there is fighting at all. Our goal is to end the war and gain harmony. When a husband and wife together seek this harmony, they then together can seek God on His way of handling the issues. We need to clearly decide that we no longer want to make our selfish desires our priority. Those desires have been destroying our marriages.

The couple is one, not two. As husband and wife, are we not on the same team? Do we not have the same goal? Are we not both winning when the other does well? We sure are! We will now look into a passage that leads us to take positive steps to implement this God-promised harmony!

B) Creating Marital Harmony (Philippians 2:1-5)

God, the great Reconciler, coaches us on conflict resolution through His words (found in the Bible). We unfortunately are not very aware of His solutions. Philippians 2:1-11 is better known for theological statements than for dealing with issues like personal problems, but this I believe was its original purpose. Christ modeled what He wants lived out in our own lives. We will limit our discussion to the first five verses.

"If therefore there is any encouragement in Christ, if there is any consolation of love, if there is any fellowship of the Spirit, if any affection and compassion, make my joy complete by being of the same mind, maintaining the same love, united in spirit, intent on one purpose. Do nothing from selfishness or empty

conceit, but with humility of mind let each of you regard one another as more important than himself; do not merely look out for your own personal interests, but also for the interests of others. Have this attitude in yourselves which was also in Christ Jesus" (Philippians 2:1-5).

This passage is almost the opposite of what we just looked at in James 4. Here we have positive steps to preserve our unity. The context is again on how the members of the church should respond to each other in light of Christ's grace and example. This might sound rather theoretical at first, but in fact it is extremely practical. With each observation below, we will apply it practically to marriage as we did before. These are things you want to do. Most likely you do some of them already but have not yet understood how vital they are to a great marriage.

1) Embrace oneness.

"By being of the same mind, maintaining the same love, united in spirit, intent on one purpose"(Philippians 2:2).

We see an inordinate emphasis placed on the life principle of oneness in Philippians 2:2. '*Same mind*,' '*same love*,' '*united in spirit*,' '*one purpose*' are all based on being of one body. This concept of oneness should become a concept so deeply rooted in our hearts that it influences how we think (thoughts), care for others (heart and attitude) and make decisions (will).

PHYSICAL ONENESS
SOUL ONENESS
SPIRITUAL ONENESS

Marriage principle: Our commitment to our spouse comes from our marriage covenant and God's declaration that the "two shall be one." Our spouse is not just another person that we live with but is part of me. What happens to him or her directly affects one's own life. In all of our decisions we must think of our spouse's well-being. As we grow in our intimate relationship with our spouse, we will gain a similar mindset, but regular preferential treatment of the other and common outlook on life deepens this intimacy. A great marriage works as a team. Husband and wife are that team and win as they work together.[43]

* FOLLOWTHROUGH *

Think through last week's significant actions and decisions.

+ Did you talk or pray about these issues with your spouse?

+ Did you share with your spouse special scripture that God has been using to speak to you?

2) Reject any impulse to selfishness.

"Do nothing from selfishness or empty conceit"
(Philippians 2:3).

Paul refuses to hide sin. He names selfishness and vain conceit for what it is. Each is a hidden motivator. Selfishness produces actions and words which supposedly bring about better results at the expense of the other, in this case, your spouse. Conceit on the other hand is high esteem for oneself combined with prideful disdain for others. Conceit hides guilt from selfishness, justifying its action in a swarm of unholy lies such as, "I can use this for God better than he can." "I've been a Christian longer than him." "I've read a lot more than he has." "He has so many problems. What does he know?"

Marriage principle: We need to hate everything associated with selfishness. Our pride makes it easier to spot our selfishness. When we see our spouse respond with despair, aggravation, debate or selfishness over something we did. *"You did what?"* We often have a whole set of excuses

---

[43] We have our share of sibling conflict in our home, but sometimes there are moments of grace that move my heart. God provided this illustration of oneness, "My best is your best." My four year-old boy and two year-old daughter just walked into my study. He was telling his little sister about his mini car collection, "Who wants to start picking first? You or me." She said, "Me." He then happily agreed saying, "Okay! You pick first." They happily played together.

prepared to disarm our spouse's antagonistic reactions. Instead of rebuffing them, respond with a humble, "Perhaps you are right. Let me think and pray more about it." Or "Let's talk more about it tonight?" Make sure you follow through.

* FOLLOWTHROUGH *
Think through last week's significant actions and decisions.

+ Did your spouse react strongly to something you did or said this past week? What was it? How did you respond?

+ In light of what was discussed above, how could you have responded?

3) Devote yourselves in humble service to each other.

"But with humility of mind let each of you regard one another as more important than himself"
(Philippians 2:3).

We rarely hear anyone applauding humility today, but Jesus and the Apostle Paul did. Not only must we be willing to carry out humble activities, but we also need to carry them out with a humble spirit. Our hearts' attitude towards serving others needs to be changed. We need to sincerely believe that the other person is more important than ourself. If we subtly denigrate their value, then it is easy to treat them pridefully. But if we value them as God's special creatures made in His image, then we must treat their needs with the utmost respect.

We must not bypass the question of whether our spouse really is more important. We must work this through. Changed actions and responses only come with new perspectives. With Christ as our example, we must treat people more special than they deserve as our life duty.

Since God treated us with grace, we are obliged and able to treat others with His kindness.

Marriage principle: Humility allows us to drop our defensive guard. Suddenly, your goal to meet the needs of your mate has become more important than protecting your ego or satisfying your own pleasures. Your goal is now to serve your mate so that he or she is blessed by your presence. Humility naturally melts away argumentative and defensive attitudes. When you are humble, you are ready to see yourself as God sees you. Equally important, you are ready to do what God has called you to do as a husband or wife. You are glad to serve God and others including your spouse.

* FOLLOWTHROUGH *

Think through last week's significant actions and decisions.

+ Were you at any point humble of heart? What makes you think this so?

+ Isolate one problem between you and your spouse. Humble yourself regarding this. Trust God for the results.

+ At an appropriate time request your spouse to share whether you had a humble spirit about this matter. Note the reaction.

4) Make a conscious effort not to watch out for your own personal needs.

"Do not merely look out for your own personal interests. (Philippians 4:4)

The word *merely* is italicized in the NASB because there is no word for it in the original. The translators inserted it. The NIV does the same thing, but they don't tell you.[44] The verse clearly commands us "Don't

---

[44] The NIV doesn't mark out their 'supplied' words. Note Philippians 2:4a, "Each of you should look not only to your own interests." The 'not only' is supplied. The passage simply tells us not to look to out for our own interests.

look out for your own personal interests." The word 'look out' comes from the Greek word *skopeo* from which our English word 'scope' is derived. Don't fix your eyes upon your own needs.[45] How desperately we need to apply this lesson to our lives.

Disobedience to this one command causes us to make many excuses for our selfishness. We can only do one or the other. God wants us to purposely focus on caring for the other person's needs. How many times have you held back God's prompting of love or giving because you thought too much about your own needs? Our neglect leaves a trail of shame and pain.

Marriage principle: The husband and wife have their God-defined commands, which at times can make them feel rather vulnerable. "If I do that, then he (or she) might...." God does not bring that thought of risk to your mind, the evil one does. Satan is tempting you. He plays on your selfishness and fears in order to influence you to disobey God. Christ's example showed how obedience is always more important than one's own welfare. In Jesus' case, it did cost Him His life but even then God worked the best through Christ's sacrifice. God said, "Don't look out for your own personal interests." We need to trust the Lord with the results.

* FOLLOWTHROUGH *

Think through last week's significant actions and decisions.

+ Did you feel prompted to do something this week for your spouse? Did you do it? Why or why not?

---

[45] We understand that there is an 'also' in the second clause of this sentence which gives some need to care for one's own needs. I see this is not a permission to modify the command of the first clause but to keep us from getting extreme with it. In other words, I don't stop taking baths or working. I just expect that God will care for my needs as I would care for God's. We of course need to carry out hygienic measures, etc. The command stands against any preference of self over others.

> ✦ Does the "If I do that, then he (or she) might…." play a factor in your decisions? Explain.

5) Commit yourself to think about the needs and interests of others.

"But also for the interests of others" (Philip 4:4).

We are to seriously rearrange our lifestyle and choices so that we can better give consideration to the needs of others. I was sick last Sunday. One brother found out. On Monday he gave me a call to find out how I was doing. Perhaps it was a professional call because he is my doctor. I didn't take it as that though. I felt his concern and care. He made a call. Rarely do I hear of a doctor calling their patients today. But even if it was, he has implanted this focus on caring for the interests or needs of others as part of his profession. God's love brightly shone through his phone call. This morning when I cut a grapefruit, I also thought about my wife and cut the small sections for her.

Marriage principle: Each spouse must make him or herself available to serve the other in any special way that God prompts. I know my

The word 'scope' is derived from the Greek word *skopeo* meaning 'look out for.'

wife is responsible to care for certain needs around the home. God has appointed her to keep the house and children.[46] But I try to make it easy for her. I take down our dirty laundry. I vacuum our bedroom floor (though not regularly enough). I try to put my clothes away (even though I fold my sweaters backwards). I try to use our once a week date

---

[46] 1 Timothy 5:14 addresses widows, who should remarry but can be understood to apply to all wives. "Therefore, I want younger *widows* to get married, bear children, keep house, *and* give the enemy no occasion for reproach" (1 Timothy 5:14).

to drive her to a few places that she would not otherwise easily get to. I don't count the time I spend with her talking and praying at night. I try to think of her needs. Lately, I have been asking her if there is a 'to do' list she would like to give me (talk about being vulnerable).

* FOLLOWTHROUGH *

Think through last week's significant actions and decisions.

- ✦ What practical steps have you taken to make life special for your spouse?

- ✦ Would you say that you treat your spouse more special because he or she is more important than yourself? How can you practically improve your attitude?

6) Glory in having an attitude toward life like Christ.

> *"Have this **attitude** in yourselves which was also in Christ Jesus" (Philippians 2:5).*

Attitudes change actions. Beliefs change behavior. We are called to possess Christ's attitude and nothing less. We are to get excited about God's calling for us in Christ because we get to join Christ in doing.' Our purpose is the same. We want to bring glory to God and help our neighbors. Seek out each day the opportunities He has brought into your life, even though at times they are very challenging.[47] By faith we live in His presence and with His help carry out what we need to.

Marriage principle: Each spouse needs to focus on improving his or her own attitudes. We must not take up the other's responsibilities when they slack off but look for ways to make it easier for the other to carry out his or her own responsibilities. This cultivates the joy of life. We

---

[47] Ephesians 2:10 is powerfully clear about God's interaction with us in each part of our day, right down to the opportunities to provide good works for us to do to glorify Him and for the sake of others. "For we are His workmanship, created in Christ Jesus for good works, which God prepared beforehand, that we should walk in them" (Ephesians 2:10).

must serve without thinking of reward. Our reward is the joy of service and allowing Jesus to be part of our marriage.[48] Sometimes a husband might be stubborn in his pride or a wife ensnared in her depressed feelings. The other spouse should not be easily offended but rather view this as a special situation where one can show Jesus' love to the other. It might take longer than we like for the other to turn around, but do your best and trust the results to God.

* FOLLOWTHROUGH *
Think through last week's significant actions and decisions.

+ Is there a situation in which your spouse is being difficult? Write it down.

+ Make a plan to love your spouse with Christ's love, especially in a difficult situation. Prepare yourself over the long term. Our hope is for God's love to finally melt down any resistance. Our contentment is found in a growing love for God and our love showered upon our spouse. Jesus stated that Mary's unselfish act of anointing His feet would be repeated throughout the generations (Mark 14:9).

Summary

We can see from the powerful example of Christ how we can begin to live out these principles in our marriages. All of these principles are built on God's proclamation that as a married couple we are one and no longer two. Therefore we must live out that fact by practical steps, some of which are outlined above.

Possible Responses

Let me anticipate some different responses to the principles we have been gathering from God's Word.

---

[48] Our end joy must be to please God, for otherwise we will be disappointed. Paul says, "Rejoice in the Lord always."

• **Resistance.** You might sense a strong feeling of resistance to these teachings. It might be a protective covering through which you hide your shortcomings when they are being exposed. Don't be afraid of the Spirit of God. His ways are good. Through Christ you can find forgiveness for all sins. If you harden yourself, there are no ways to improve your marriage. Many marriages have shamefully broken apart because partners have hardened themselves.

• **Shame.** You might feel a lot of shame. It is hard when we, like cancer, have brought damage to our own body (i.e. our spouse). Just think, we could have used those same days, months and years to bring Christ's love. God forgives and empowers us as we humbly turn to Him.

• **Shock.** You might be shocked at how long you have been in the church and yet never connected God's Word with these life principles. All of a sudden you see them applying to your marriage. You wonder, "How could I have missed God's message of love?" You are not the first or the last that this will happen to. Thank the Lord that His forgiveness is complete and is willing to work with any humble soul.

• **Argumentative.** You might have an argument stirring within you to contest something that has been said. We are not afraid of the questions. God's truth always leads to the best life. Such questions more often than not attempt to disguise one's guilt. Focus on what God has taught you. Clarify the principles and carry them out. Be open to the possibility of your guilt and confess your sin.

• **Too ideal.** 'Too ideal' is one of those quick excuses that glosses over either our personal guilt or refusal to obey. If a person sincerely believes it is beyond his reach but would like to aspire to it, then it would be better to rephrase the thought, "I want to be like that but haven't been able. I wonder if you have some suggestions for how I could achieve that."

• **Yes!** This is the way we would like couples to take the Lord's teaching. "Oh yes, that is what we have been looking for in our marriage for a long time! Pray for us so that we can put this into operation." Is this your response? If not, why not?

Summary

Now let us assemble together all the principles that we have learned in this section. The source of all quarrels and conflicts is right in our own selfish hearts. The sad part is that we have hurt the ones that we are supposed to love, sometimes for many years. The good part is that we have a Savior Jesus who is greater than our sins. The power of Christ can set us free to have a Christ-like attitude of humble service. As long as the self-serving spirit governs us, there is no chance for peace. A person's selfishness will compete against Christ's giving spirit.

If one person is gracious, then the marriage will instantly improve, but it will still be difficult. Would it not be better to have both spouses committed to carrying out Christ-like attitudes and actions? God is willing to teach us. He has been all along.

He is with us today. He is listening to what our hearts are saying. Is it a cry, "Oh God, help me be like you!" God has a plan to help those with that cry. God will answer your prayer. Trust Him and begin a notebook to keep track of how God rebuilds your marriage.

Here is a sample prayer.

Dear Lord, I have never realized how far our marriage has been off track. I thought we were above average. I now see that we are far from where you want to take us. Lord, please forgive me of my sin. I have failed many times without even realizing it. Sometimes I am aware of my selfishness but was too stubborn to make amends. O, make my heart tender. Break my love for self and pride that keeps us from having a great marriage.

The war is over. From this time on I declare a truce. I am now for peace. I choose your love and your presence. I want our home to be a place Jesus would be welcome in all the time. I know I have a long way to go, but you can help me. I might not be the sole cause for all the arguing in our home, but I know I am very large part of it. Please forgive me. Let me not fear humility but embrace it as Jesus has.

May I be a wonderful spouse. Please give us a great marriage, Lord. We don't deserve a great marriage after all that has gone on. But you are merciful. You are powerful. Do your work in our marriage to your glory. In Christ's Name I pray, Amen.

Chapter #5 Study Questions

1. Is it possible to have a peaceful home? How?

2. What were the last two things that you argued about with your spouse?

3. What two words are discussed from James 4:1-3? How do they differ?

4. Why do we need to go below the surface when dealing with conflicts?

5. What can I do as one spouse to bring great improvement to my marriage?

6. What causes the actual harm in conflict? Why is this so?

7. What do you say to the spouse who says, "I can't help it."

8. Why don't selfish spouses ask God to help them?

9. How can wealth bring harm to a marriage?

10. How can a commitment to the oneness principle help your marriage in a practical sense?

11. Is it really possible to "Do nothing from selfishness or empty conceit?" Provide one practical example of this from your marriage.

12. What does 'humbling oneself' mean? How does it help a marriage?

13. Why should the phrase, "If I do that, then he (or she) might...." alert me to temptation?

14. A spouse has two choices of whom to serve. What are they? What is the end result of each?

15. Think through how Jesus dealt with people in the Gospels. What is Christ's attitude like?

16. Write down one or two ways the Spirit is prompting you to apply these Biblical principles. State the date when you will start implementing them.

Building a
Great Marriage

#6 Resolving Crises & Avoiding Conflicts

Marital Conflict Resolution: Part 2

Why do couples fight and argue? Why can't they just enjoy lasting peace? Didn't they get married to have a greater life together than when they were single?

A) The Problem-solving Process

Last night my wife and I were speaking about a certain topic. We disagreed. I saw no problem with going ahead with filling out an application for something. She was hesitant. I asked her the typical, "Why?" and she answered her typical, "I don't know why." I could have continued on and mentioned that because she did not know what the problem was, there was no real problem to carrying out what I thought was good.

I knew I was right so I could proceed with the application. But we have learned a lot over the years.

There are three basic steps to solving these differences: disagree, discuss and decide.

When we find that we disagree about something, we slow down. We put off decisions and start praying. I begin questioning her more carefully

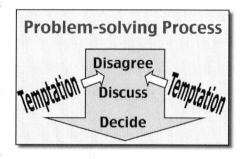

at different times about why she thinks a certain way. Sometimes she is clearer than at other times. That is fine. I value her input. I seek her insight.

In fact I am so convinced that God will speak to me through her at times that I become reluctant to proceed while she feels hesitant. If we both desire God's will, then God should speak to both of us. I don't just use my authority as a husband to make decisions. God has appointed her as my helpmate. It is the husband's responsibility to make sure the best decision pleasing to God is made. At times, She is more in tune with God and His ways than I am. This becomes an opportunity to learn more about God, His ways and each other. I resist the tendency to rely on my pride and rather get excited about what God might be saying through my wife even if I am not sure of it being best.

The difference that we had in this case had all of the ingredients for a good argument. I took one step toward doing something that she didn't feel comfortable about. (I thought I had communicated clearly about the matter). I could have stuck firmly to my path, and she could have resisted. Instead we have focused on God's will and have been praying about and discussing the issue together. As of this writing the issue is a bit clearer but not yet resolved. That is okay. Seeking God's way of resolving these differences is as important as finding the right solution.

I have recently been carefully observing our relationship as we encounter personal differences. We had four differences: over insurance, schooling and two on the discipline of our children. Sounds normal, doesn't it? In each case we had significant disagreement. Maybe one person was agitated at times. And yet we didn't argue.

In our last chapter, we showed the general approach to resolving major marital quarrels. If we first try to handle individual conflicts or 'battles,' then our solutions will be superficial and will not work. Couples need a new approach to marriage. They need to see that they are on the same team and therefore resolve to:

➡ (1) Deliberately refuse to oppose each other, and

➡ (2) Design the means to work together toward a great marriage.

The typical married couple allows far too much room for the evil one to bring harm to their marriage. We should not allow this. If we find ourselves fighting with our spouses, we should take note of the willingness in our hearts to battle and repent from this fighting spirit. Conflict reveals an impure heart. Spouses must be convinced that when they  beat, subdue or take advantage of their spouse that both of them have lost. As a married couple we are a team, and we aim to make that team a success!

Once we have this basic commitment toward our spouse, we can then take a deeper look at the conflicts couples face. Perhaps a good illustration of this is when a truce is made. Each side can stop fighting. In the old days of poor communication, battles sometimes went on for days even after the war was called off! Hasn't the war been called off in our marriage? Do we still need to have conflicts if peace has been made? No. Do we still have them? Yes, we do, but they are no longer necessary. There is a better way of handling differing opinions.

We need a very clear way to resolve these varying opinions or the enemy will use them to make us think that we are at war with each other. This in turn results in setting up opposing sides (which is counter to the oneness principle). Differences in opinion are not wrong, but if we are not careful, they will become battlefields. Look at opinions as opportunities to gain more insight into some issue.

Someone might say that their chief problems are not with disagreements but just with emotional reactions. For example the husband comes home cranky or the wife barrages her husband at the door with a slew of problems as he enters.[49] Let us make a few observations.

What are normally called emotional problems, more often than not, are rooted in spiritual problems. Our emotions are closely intertwined with our spiritual natures. If we do not properly handle an offense, then we can easily become angered. If not dealt with, we will bring that anger home and get irritated with our spouse.

Every argument requires two sides. Even if one spouse is upset, it does not mean that there needs to be a battle. The other spouse needs to carefully monitor the situation with a prayerful and patient spirit.

Every spiritual problem that we do not properly resolve will inject poison into our marriage. The husband and wife live too closely together not to be affected by personal sin. Sin reveals itself in our marriage.

---

[49] We acknowledge there are physical changes that affect a person's ability to respond as normal. Still God says His grace is sufficient. We should look for extra grace in such times. Meanwhile the spouse must be extra loving.

The power of the gospel sets us free from those sins. We do not need to allow worries, fears, doubts, anger, hate, etc. control us. Christ can forgive us as the Spirit empowers us.

Remain Focused on Ministry

We need to orient our lives around ministering to others, including our spouses on their bad days. The Spirit of God wants to use us to intercede and express His love to our spouse. Even though our spouse might be impatient, we need to patiently care for him or her.

In a good way, both the husband and wife should check their attitudes and lives before encountering each other. Ask yourself, "Am I in a state in which God can minister His love and grace through my life to my spouse." If not, ask Him to prepare you and wait until He does!

Lastly, we should remember, that the disagreement we are referring to is not necessarily a verbal disagreement. A difference in approach toward a situation or the expectation of another can also bring about the same volatile situation. If a husband leaves a dirty sock laying around, it just might be enough to set a couple against each other. The husband sees it as no big deal. The wife is convinced the sock should not be there. Perhaps she thinks he purposely left it there to bother her! In such cases there are deeper problems behind the scenes.

People will always have differences of opinions and approaches. This is true with couples too. What we do with these dissimilar viewpoints is what will characterize our lives and marriages. Great marriages are those that have learned how to utilize these differences so they can grow as a couple. Poor marriages, however, mishandle these differing perspectives and bring further trouble to their relationships.

Keeping away from strife is an honor for a man, but any fool will quarrel (Proverbs 20:3).

We need to realize that conflicts are more than the simple difference of opinion. Conflicts are the way couples poorly advance their varying viewpoints. Spouses can get quite mean and cruel at times. On the other hand, we can see that these crises also serve as opportunities to draw closer to God and closer to our spouse.

The Book of Joshua was partly written to help us better understand how to handle ourselves during these crises. If we carefully pay attention to God's instructions to the Israelites, then we will better understand how to turn these potential arguments into times of growth, mutual love and trust. Doesn't that sound like a much more pleasant way to spend an evening? Rightly responding to differences leads to a great marriage.

B) Resolving Crises (Joshua)

There are six ways Joshua worked with God during a crisis to avoid conflict.

(1) Crises enable us to affirm our oneness

In a sense, when Israel went into the Promised Land, they could say that the war was already over. This might sound crazy, but it was true. God said He had given the land to them. He furthermore said that no one would be able to stand against them. When God is on your side, then the war is over.

> *"Every place on which the sole of your foot treads, I have given it to you, just as I spoke to Moses. ... No man will be able to stand before you all the days of your life. Just as I have been with Moses, I will be with you; I will not fail you or forsake you"* (Joshua 1:3,5).

Do you remember Jericho? All they had to do was walk around it. God told them how to win without losing. These things are true not only for our Christian lives, but also for our marriages. The biggest hurdle for a couple to overcome is simply the determination not to fight.

They need to realize that the battle is already won. They are on the same team. God has proclaimed them one for life.

Because of our human desires, we will still have misunderstandings, differing opinions, selfish times, lazy moments, etc., but we must learn how to properly respond to our spouse and manage our own attitudes. These misunderstandings will occur. We will have crises, but the war is over, and since the war is over, we can approach these differences with a completely different heart and approach.

When God is on your side, the war is over!

I have dealt with couples in both situations. When husband and wife are contesting for their rights, there is no way to settle their conflict. I suppose there are laws and rules one can put in place, but once a person is offended, he or she will continue to misunderstand the other person's motives. There is no easy cure once mistrust takes root.

When, however, the couple is working together as one, these differences are almost fun to solve. We get to really work on the problem before God. We get to see how God is going to intervene and help clarify the situation as we call upon Him. Our marriage grows as we solve things together.

- What do you argue about as a couple?
- Why do you argue?
- How long have you argued about the same thing?

(2) Crises point out our potential problems

When couples are fighting, conflicts are almost impossible to solve. There is too much angst, too much selfishness. But when that whole sphere of infighting is removed, then we get to see God work.

We should be aware that marriage is the chief context in which God works out His sanctification purposes in our lives. He is making us to be more and more like Jesus. Crises are signs that God wants to develop certain areas of our lives. This was true for the crises that Joshua and the Israelite armies faced too. Let's look at a few of these illustrative passages.

"Now it came about when Adoni-zedek king of Jerusalem heard that Joshua had captured Ai, and had utterly destroyed it (just as he had done to Jericho and its king, so he had done to Ai and its king), ... that he feared greatly, therefore Adoni-zedek king of Jerusalem sent word to Hoham king of Hebron ... saying, "Come up to me and help me, and let us attack Gibeon, for it has made peace with Joshua and with the sons of Israel" (Joshua 10:1-4).

"Do not fear them" (Joshua 10:8)

"Do not be afraid because of them" (Joshua 11:6).

"Then it came about, when Jabin king of Hazor heard of it, ... And they came out, they and all their armies with them, as many people as the sand that is on the seashore, with very many horses and chariots. So all of these kings having agreed to meet, came and encamped together at the waters of Merom, to fight against Israel" (Joshua 11:1-5).

Each time the enemy raised his ugly head, the Lord comforted the Israelites, "Do not fear them" (Joshua 10:8) or "Do not be afraid because of them" (Joshua 11:6). The question was not whether they would win. God spoke to them so that they would be able to trust Him for victory as He led them into battle. God wants us to enter these crises with the same confidence. God is in control. Trust in Him. God furthermore explained to Joshua the secret of why they needed to go through these crises.

"For it was of the LORD to harden their hearts, to meet Israel in battle in order that he might utterly destroy them, that they might receive no mercy,

but that he might destroy them, just as the LORD had commanded Moses" *(Joshua 11:20).*

God at times would exaggerate the crises by hardening the heart of the enemy. The king in turn would get other kings to join in the fight. God's purpose was simple. God wanted the enemy eliminated as quickly and cleanly as possible. (By the way, our spouse is not the enemy!) This is the same for our lives too. Even though as couples we run into what can be big disagreements, they are not really any different than smaller disagreements. The solution is the same.

Greater trust is needed for greater intimacy. The Lord is building a great marriage. We can expect crises to propel us further into that closeness.

God works through these times. He knows deep down that there are areas we have not fully turned over to Him. He wants His love to dominate those areas. These are usually bad attitudes and unloving actions that we have learned from our parents. We at times don't even know of any other way to handle a certain situation other than the way our parents have shown us. (Are we not often ignorant of our major flaws?) God, however, is not pleased with such responses.

When a couple sees a disagreement coming up between themselves, it is much like what Joshua saw when looking at his intimidating enemies. There is potential for danger if not properly handled. However, if we work it through the way God leads us, then we will achieve victory, and God will bring about a special work of purification in our hearts.

We should not be afraid of a crisis or be intimidated by it. Our feelings might be aroused and urge us to rush in and solve it 'our' way, but we must reject these feelings. We are in no hurry. The issue is not whether we can overcome, but how the Lord is going to help resolve it. The key is to join together in seeking God's solution. In the event the situation seems impossible, remember that God used all sorts of unusual ways to solve the crises Joshua faced: hail, long days, confusion and even cornets. Life was supernatural. The same will be true for our marriage as we seek Him in these crises.

When we begin to see how God works with us to solve our crises, it becomes easier to think of the husband and wife as a team working with God. Moreover, we see God 'growing' us. We begin to get excited about how God is working in us. We are on the same winning team.

God's ultimate purpose is peace, purity and rest. God was willing, however, to bring confrontation to reach that goal of harmony. The same is true with our marriage. God does not tempt us, but He does test us. The test is our opportunity to live by trust in Him, trusting that He wants to do something special in our circumstances. Crises arise to help us know that we have not yet obtained the harmony God has promised us. We have not yet gained all that God wants us to have. We have a promise of it. We like it. But we have a bit more work to do in order to obtain it.

• What was your last crisis?

• Do you find that difference of opinions always leads to arguments?

• Do you have times when differing ideas do not lead to conflict? Explain.

(3) Crises often build upon past unresolved conflict

Some couples find that they always argue. Crises almost always lead to conflict. In such cases, each spouse needs to step back and complete a personal conflict inventory.

Conflicts often have very long histories. When a couple has regularly given into conflict, then it is obvious they have accepted a sinful

"Visiting the iniquity of the fathers on the children, on the third and the fourth generations of those who hate Me" (Exodus 20:5).

Great grandparents   Great grandparents
⬇   ⬇
Grandparents   Grandparents
⬇   ⬇
Parents   Parents
⬇   ⬇
Husband   Wife

Each spouse can be significantly impacted by their forefathers' sins. When the couple gets married, they are also intermixing their sins!

way of handling differences. God has a better way. The issue, however, is a bit trickier to solve.

More than likely, these inclinations to use conflict in discussions have been passed on for generations. For example, if you can trace an adulterous heart in your parents and grandparents, then more than likely you have the same struggle of being completely devoted to your spouse. If your parents argued, then you have learned that it is normal to argue. You have not only learned to argue, but you have learned the attitude behind the argument: "I am right; you are wrong!" But let us turn this around. Instead of looking at your parents' faults, take a look at your own marriage.

Personal Reflections

What problems do you have a difficult time handling? Try to isolate a few areas. They might include handling money, facing disappointment, or using anger[50] to intimidate your spouse to get what you want. Now take a close look at your parents and see if they also had the same kind of problems. Remember, do not only examine their personal sins but carefully observe how they related to their spouses and children. What do you find?

God wanted the Israelites to eliminate long-standing enemies. He wanted them to live in a holy manner and conduct themselves in love according to His laws. Those nations, however, were secure in the land. They had their strongholds. The Israelites were coming in to take over the land these Amorites controlled. They lived in strong fortresses. Some, like Jerusalem, were located on a hard-to-reach mountain (Judges 1:21). They were hard to root out.

Joshua, however, was willing to look at these strong enemies from God's perspective. He knew it wasn't his personal project that would conquer Canaan. God had His own purposes. That is why they were going to win. God laid out His plan of attack four hundred years earlier!

Then in the fourth generation they shall return here, for the iniquity of the Amorite is not yet complete"
(Genesis 15:16).

Joshua might have purposed deep in his heart to fight the enemy, but he also had to learn how to work with God to accomplish these plans. The means to carry out these plans are just as important as our goals. Fighting marital struggles through our self-efforts only leads to defeat in the end even if we achieve initial success. We cannot win by overpowering or outwitting our spouse. Will power is not going to give us great marriages.

---

[50] God can cure anger! Refer to
www.foundationsforfreedom.net/Topics/Anger/Anger00.html .

Instead we need to see that God had already decided to eliminate the enemy. Joshua knew he could lead the Israelites to conquer because God had predetermined it. We as couples also know that God is in the business of giving us great marriages. We need to eliminate those bad responses to get there. He sets up opportunities for us to grow and win.

God did not bring all the enemies to Joshua at once. He started with Jericho to encourage and train them. It was only later that God could work more quickly by bringing more enemies at once to conquer. God never brings us too much too handle if we trust in Him. We spouses also have a large reservoir of potential self-expressions that will bring harm to our marriage. Let us think a little bit more about how these 'enemies' threaten our harmony.

Some of these 'enemies' are jealousy, worry, fear, pride, hatred and covetousness. They literally destroy marriages. Every time they have an opportunity, they will coax us into wrongly handling a certain situation. They intimidate us into making poor decisions. In a similar way, Israel's enemy armies sometimes formed coalitions to better intimidate and beat Israel. We might feel these forces are strong, but God's purposes are greater and more glorious. This is why it is crucial that we personally meet God each day early in the morning so that we can be in tune to Him and His purposes.

The tensions and struggles that appear from a difference of opinion do not need to turn into conflict. When spouses are willing to follow

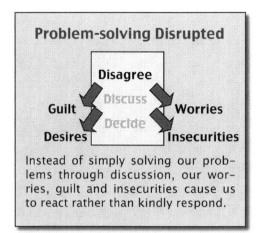

Problem-solving Disrupted

Disagree

Guilt   Discuss   Worries

Decide

Desires   Insecurities

Instead of simply solving our problems through discussion, our worries, guilt and insecurities cause us to react rather than kindly respond.

their natural inclinations, they will end up in a big argument. This is conflict. The Lord did not give a marriage two minds to argue but to provide greater wisdom and insight which results in more stability.

Our marriage will only be as strong as the work we put into each of these areas with our spouse. Marriages grow as the spouses grow spiritually. Marriage is the place where God brings us to where He wants us to be.

Once lower standards are tolerated, which are not standards at all, we bring pain and conflict into our marriages. The exciting part is that God is patiently working with us. He is there to eliminate the enemy. Peace is secured as we conquer. Praise God for how He works to help us as individuals and couples overcome these crises. Where once we were crippled, now we are strong!

Personal Reflections

- What personal struggles do you battle with? Do you see these struggles at all in your parent's relationship or the way they handle different situations? Explain.

- Marriage is a context through which God works out our personal issues and sins. Ask God to further purge these wrong responses from you. Look to Him to cleanse, instruct and master the right responses.

(4) Crises must be solved God's way

Conflicts need to cease. Fortunately, God has given us a pattern by which the enemies that we meet during crises can be overcome. We find these secrets to victory in the battles recorded in Joshua. The pattern goes something like this: A crisis leads His people to call on His Name which in turn allows God to speak. With God's plan and help, they secure victory. The Israelites seek the Lord, and the Lord faithfully leads them to victory, time after time.

Crisis develops ➡ **Call on the Lord** ➡ **Calm down** ➡ **Careful planning** ➡ **Complete victory**

Someone might ask what happened at Ai where Israel was overcome by the enemy? Good question. Joshua failed to ask God for direction before the battle. Of course it was sad that someone had also violated God's special prohibition. If Joshua had talked to the Lord about the matter rather than presuming victory, God would have prevented that disaster. Victory (such as at Jericho) can lead to pride and there seems to be some problem of self-confidence at this stage.

God's advice and direction when implemented always leads to victory. Now let's ask a question. Do you want to have a great marriage or not? The only way to establish a strong marriage is to constantly seek God. "And the Lord said to Joshua, "See, I have given Jericho into your hand, with its king and the valiant warriors" (Joshua 6:2). Only God has the answers to the problems we face.

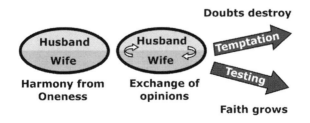

Jericho was a heavily guarded city with huge intimidating double walls. Our greatest problem is that when we first sense a difference of opinion, we do not immediately turn to the Lord. What does it mean to follow the Lord? The following diagrams will clarify what seeking God means and why it works.

There are several stages to this.[51] The key is to remember that we all start off at the same place in front of the altar where we happily pledge ourselves to each other in marriage. Things are fine. Everything is peaceful. It is only when we sense a difference of opinion or varied approach to some matter that we begin to sense the crisis. It is here that both temptation and testing come in. James 1 instructs us on the difference between them.

Temptation	*Testing*
Let no one say when he is tempted, "I am being tempted by God"; for God cannot be tempted by evil, and He Himself does not tempt anyone. But each one is tempted when he is carried away and enticed by his own lust; Then when lust has conceived, it gives birth to sin (James 1:13-15).	Consider it all joy, my brethren, when you encounter various trials, knowing that the testing of your faith produces endurance. Blessed is a man who perseveres under trial; for once he has been approved, he will receive the crown of life, which the Lord has promised to those who love Him (Jam 1:2-3,12).

Temptation is from the evil one. He purposes to divide and split. This is the opposite of responding to the truth of oneness. He does it by emphasizing differences and giving us plenty of opportunity to get 'carried away' by our own lusts. His hope is that we would hurt each other resulting in long-term scars. He attempts to get us to say bad things

---

[51] A more thorough treatment is at www.foundationsforfreedom.net/ Topics/Family/Parenting009_Harmony.html

about our spouse and then make us conclude that it is best to act on these things (even if we really did not mean it).

Personal Reflections

What are some of the unwholesome things you have said? "I will never speak to her again." "I hate you." Make sure you identify and own up to your bad words, confess them and seek apology. Be as specific as possible.

Conflict is never good because it always leads down a bad road. Some counselors call conflict normal. It is not. God never considers unkind words and acts as normal. He told us to "speak the truth in love."

Testing is from God. Crises are occasions to emphasize our oneness. We have decided to follow the Lord. When we face some difference, we seek the Lord out in prayer and arrange times to further discuss the issue with our spouse. When sensing an upset spirit, put it down by deciding not to follow it. This is done by recognizing it (before it breeds trouble), rejecting it and affirming your oneness by some practical deed. You might say, "Honey, I know we disagree on this issue, but let's talk and pray together about it later when we both have more time." Words can be very affirming.

Consciously choose to work together to see what God wants for your family. When you see what God wants, then each of you can make the necessary adjustments to his or her life to accommodate what God wants. Temptation (from the evil one) and testing (from God) become the two options at every point of disagreement. Notice them and choose God's way.

The Degenerating Cycle

What happens when the couple responds to the temptation? In the adjacent diagram, we see that the choice to follow temptation brings about terrible consequences. It always brings harm to the relationship and sometimes painful wounds. If clear improvement does not come about, a degenerating cycle takes place and cements this cycle of negative responses into the marriage. Instead of overcoming the enemy, they give into the wishes of the enemy and adjust their lives to this daily dose of affliction.

Many marriages are plagued by this degenerating cycle. By degenerating it means that the marriage gets worse and worse each time the couple goes through a 'fight' cycle. We are not saying that it cannot get better, but it requires a genuine humbling of the soul to apologize and get things straight. More will be said on forgiveness in the next chapter.

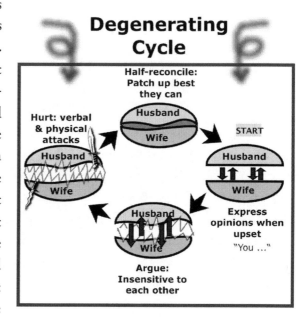

When proper apologies are not made, then a residing layer of bitterness lies between the couple (see the chart on the right). There is no perfect harmony even when they are not arguing. When another argument starts, the couple continues where they last left off. This degenerating cycle repeats because bitterness seeks another occasion to lash out. They no longer start at the top with nothing between them but rather with bitterness, so to speak, oiling their bitter conversations. We highly recommend another method to respond to crises that bypasses this downward spiral.

The Regenerating Cycle

The regenerating cycle brings life rather than death into the relationship each time the cycle progresses. This cycle starts in harmony (at the top) and ends establishing a stronger marriage than ever. These gains are possible because the differing perspectives never lead into 'attack' mode. If they do, forgiveness is sought and gained.

The difference of the opposing position of the spouse is accepted for what it is. Just because two people differ, it does not mean that they

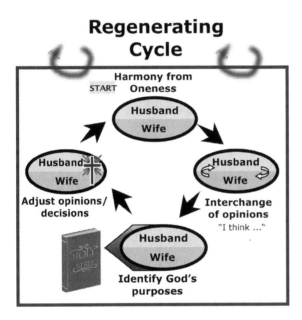

have to 'have it their way.' They both are seeking God's viewpoint and make adjusts as necessary.

A husband and wife will not always agree, even after discussion. In a later chapter we will provide a detailed explanation about how a wife and husband need to respond if there are disagreements even after carefully looking at God's Word (for example on how much they should give to the church or the poor). Mature couples are willing to solve irreconcilable differences in God's ways. It needs to be stated, however, that differences of opinion can stem from not seeking the Lord on some matter (e.g. buying a new car on credit because one does not have the money - coveting). In any case, every couple has plenty of differences to give them practice on working with their spouse to solve problems.

If a couple is going to resolve matters in God's ways, then each spouse needs to be close to God (so they can be patient), talk to each other (an impasse makes it very difficult) and desirous of God's purposes. In the end, if a couple invests time together (separate from these contentious times!), it will pay off. They will 'fight' less and win more. There are two cycles: the degenerating cycle and the regenerating one. The difference between them is like night and day. The former builds upon bitterness while the later builds up from forgiveness.

(5) Crises can lead us to great marriages

Joshua had a choice to hang around Jericho after the first battle or to continue leading Israel in battle and distributing land to each tribe. The whole land was their inheritance. They needed to capture and maintain it. The last half of the Book of Joshua emphasizes how Joshua carefully distributed lots of land to each tribe. They needed to be motivated to finish the task God had clearly given them.

> *"And there remained among the sons of Israel seven tribes who had not divided their inheritance. So Joshua said to the sons of Israel, "How long will you put off entering to take possession of the land which the LORD, the God of your fathers, has given you?" (Joshua 18:2-3)*

After a few setbacks, it is easy to enter into 'toleration' mode. We tend to accept it as an 'okay' marriage. We lack the motivation to have a great marriage. What do you think the Lord will do to prod the couple stained with a spirit of toleration? Sure enough, He will see to it that they face more crises until they finally realize that they better shape up their marriage.

"The contentions of a wife are a constant dripping"
(Proverbs 19:13)

God wants us to have harmonious and delightful marriages not only for our sake but for His glory. The glory of God was designed to shine through a husband

and wife's harmony. What was God's motive when He made Eve for Adam? Was He not thinking of something better than what Adam had before? Sure! When a man has a wife, he is blessed. When he has an excellent wife, he is greatly blessed.

> He who finds a wife finds a good thing, and obtains favor from the Lord (Proverbs 18:22).

If a wife or husband is irresponsible, then the marriage goes sour fairly quickly. Many proverbs highlight the error of a man who is lazy or irresponsible. "Keeping away from strife is an honor for a man, but any fool will quarrel" (Proverbs 20:3). Another whole group of proverbs point out the sadness of those marriages that have a cantankerous and complaining wife. These spouses have failed God and their spouses. They are self-seeking. "The contentions of a wife are a constant dripping" (Proverbs 19:13b).

We need a spirit like Caleb's. He remembered God's promise and believed God for the strength to obtain it.

Now then, give me this hill country about which the LORD spoke on that day, for you heard on that day that Anakim were there, with great fortified cities; perhaps the LORD will be with me, and I shall drive them out as the LORD has spoken (Joshua 14:12).

When we understand that the Lord really wants to give us a blessed marriage then we will rise in faith and believe Him to give us what otherwise would be impossible. We might have a lot going against us like Caleb, but his faith in God made up all the difference. "With God all things are possible!"

(6) Crises result in permanent conflict if not properly resolved

We are so sad to see how many couples do not take God's Word seriously. They insist on having power struggles. We certainly do not envy them! God has given us the possibility of eliminating these struggles. One by one as we resolve these crises, our marriages get sweeter and sweeter. The enemy is systematically eliminated. God's intention is only good. Unfortunately, we are not as thorough as God would have us be.

> *"But they did not drive out the Canaanites who lived in Gezer, so the Canaanites live in the midst of Ephraim to this day, and they became forced laborers" (Joshua 16:10, also 17:12).*

Anything not eliminated becomes an irritating sore spot in our marriages. Israel suffered constant harassment as long as they 'tolerated' the presence of the enemy in their land. If they eliminated rather than just subdued an enemy, then it would be gone and further unable to trouble them.

"God is not mocked for whatever a man sows, this he will also reap." (Galatians 6:7)

We need to remember that these compromises will not only take joy from what could be a great marriage but that these struggles will be passed down to our children. By the parents' actions and attitudes, their sad handling of conflict passes right down to their children. Paul in Galatians 6:7 says, "God is not mocked."

He isn't in the least fooled. We do not have any excuses for our disobedience. Even if we start off on the wrong foot, if we take God seriously, we can become an agent for His divine change starting with our own personal lives and marriages. Disharmony and troubles last as long as we do not conquer the enemy.

Of course, if we choose to follow the Lord, then we are able to handle these crises. It is here that intimacy develops. Intimate marriages pass on all sorts of good things to our children (e.g. like how to be patient with one another).

The means by which Joshua and the Israelites handled many crises in Canaan provides great insight into how a married couple should handle difficult times. We can respond God's way and win, or we can respond in fear or compromise and lose. There is a wrong and a right way. There is a degenerating cycle as well as a regenerating cycle. Our choices have a great impact on our marriages and even on our children. No marriage, however, is so bad that it cannot start anew. Nor is any marriage so secure that it is beyond the reach of bitterness, if it is allowed to settle in.

Conclusion

Conflict can be avoided. God has given us harmony through our oneness. In the end, each couple needs to retrain themselves so that they will discuss and pray instead of argue. Let me close with another illustration of how a 'blowup' between my wife and I was avoided.

My wife and I found out that we disagreed about what to do for homeschooling next year. I was surprised that she differed from me (shouldn't she always agree?)! I value her opinion, though. I had already talked through certain aspects of homeschooling next year with her. She obviously did not understand my intentions. Our differences persisted.

We discussed different plusses and minuses of doing things, this or that way. I gave her time to voice how these decisions would affect her schedule and routine. In the end she had a difference of opinion but couldn't clearly identify what the reasons for this were. I have learned that my wife needs extra time to identify her reasons. So instead of pushing forward the implementation of my plans, I paused. Again, a possible argument was diffused. Instead we were praying and working through the discussion over the course of several days. During our discussions, however, I spotted two major concerns.

First, she didn't have confidence in my leadership. I had not voiced how I was thinking about the issues of changing curriculum and the impact on her schedule. I calmly tried to explain how I was thinking about that matter. As I did this, she calmed down. A typical problem of husbands is to fail to discuss with their wives what they have clearly thought through. The wife might assume her husband has neglected to care for that area when in fact he has already given much thought to it.

Second, by valuing her opinions, though they differed from mine, I could, by God's grace, seek to know why what she said was important. At that time, I was, without knowing it, identifying her values. Our values typically are the same, as they were in this case.[52] She stated that she was concerned whether our children were being properly trained to gain a biblical perspective. I loved hearing that, and after that, I could more easily understand why she had insisted on a certain curriculum book. I thought the book was inadequate for what our children needed but now could suggest other ways to tackle that important aspect of training. The issue was resolved.

Most issues can be resolved when the husband and wife regularly pray and talk together. If the couple finds themselves too busy to talk and enjoy each other's company, then they will tend to argue and fuss more. A great marriage takes time, but every second is worth the while. Wouldn't you rather discuss than argue, pray instead of fighting? Isn't a kind word better than a critical one? We think so.

---

[52] When our values are different, it is easy to go to the scriptures to find common ground.

Personal Reflections

+ List the last three areas where you and your spouse had different opinions.

+ What did you differ about?

+ Were these issues resolved? How long did it take?

+ Were they properly handled? Explain.

+ What were the final results?

+ List any lessons to be learned.

Chapter #6 Study Questions

1. What are two things the husband and wife must do if they are going to have a great marriage?

2. Are conflicts necessary? Why or why not?

3. Are differences of opinions necessary? Are they wrong? How should they be handled?

4. How should we handle emotional upsets?

5. How does God use crises to 'sanctify' or make a couple more holy?

6. How are our conflicts connected to our parents and grandparents conflicts?

7. What is God's way of resolving conflict?

8. Briefly explain three out of six ways Joshua avoided conflict by working closely with God.

9. What is the difference between testing and temptation? How do they relate to a crisis and conflict?

10. Draw and explain the degenerating cycle.

11. Draw and explain the regenerating cycle.

12. What are the consequences of failing to resolve conflicts?

Building a
Great Marriage

#7 Replacing Marital Bitterness with Forgiveness

Bitterness, I believe, is the number one killer of our marriages. Many would object and say it is differences over money or incompatibility, but these people do not understand how bitterness is a root problem for these and many other marital difficulties. Bitterness, step by step, separates the couple from each other and lessens their commitment to each other.

God wants to bring healing to marriages. He wants to eliminate all resentment. Part of our problem is that we do not understand how He has already given us the tools to detach ourselves from the intimidating influence of bitterness in our marriages through the wonderful power of the Gospel. That little stone that God used in David's hand is much like the special tool that God has given to His children to take down the threatening giant of bitterness. Through our simple faith and obedience, God's powerful love will bring down the towering walls of resentment.

If we are not careful, however, resentment will arise in our hearts and assault our marriages. Instead of being the victor, we will become the victim. Those consumed by bitterness slowly watch the destruction of their marriage. Just recently I heard about a marriage in which the bitterness had grown so bad that the wife could not sleep at night. This was only one of the many symptoms of a marriage infected by bitterness. There are many others. Again and again, we see couples devastated by bitterness. It is a pity that couples wait until their marriage is on the verge of breakdown before they deal with the bitterness in their lives.

Anyone who has been infected by marital bitterness knows that it will dominate one's whole life if allowed. All sorts of physical symptoms pop up including lots of stress-related pains and diseases. But it does not stop there. Bitterness starts by destroying relationships. It begins so subtlety, though. Here are some possible symptoms of a breakdown in a relationship due to bitterness: rolling your eyes, ignoring simple requests, being easily irritated, calling names in "fun," criticizing your spouse's efforts, jesting about shortcomings and feeling put out. So many marriages have been destroyed simply by not following the apostle's simple instruction:

> *"Let all bitterness and wrath and anger and clamor and slander be put away from you, along with all malice" (Ephesians 4:31).*

Bitterness should not be accepted in our personal lives. If we refuse to tolerate it, then it would not plague our marriages. Bitterness eats away from the God-given goodness in our marriages. Why then have so many couples accepted some degree of bitterness in their marriages? Some have never thought about how bitterness is related to their troubled marriages. Others know of it, but are so clearly committed to destroying the other, that they are willing to put up with the suffering.

In our following discussion, we will explain how bitterness and anger deeply damage marriages and outline clear steps to eliminate bitterness and gain that sweet relationship that marriage is designed to be.

A) Understanding the Root of Bitterness

Marital bitterness comes from being offended by one's spouse and holding a begrudging heart against him or her. For example, a husband might say to his wife, "That meal was not very good." His intention might not be as bad as the wife feels. But in any case, the wife resents her husband's remark.

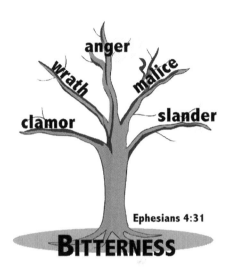

She thinks to herself how it is so easy for him to just come home and expect a grand meal. She might cover up, and yet slightly reveal, her bitterness by some gesture, inflection of voice or some private decision when making the meal. Resentment, right or wrong, has been planted in her soul, and she is responding to it.

The seed of bitterness is planted in so many ways. Instead of speaking honestly with her husband about how that comment hurt her, she secretly stores the offense in her heart and cools her heart toward him. Increasing distance between the couple will continue to produce misunderstandings until resolved.

From the verse above (Ephesians 4:31), we can see that bitterness has many 'brothers and cousins' including: wrath (i.e. temper), anger, clamor (i.e. noise), slander and malice (i.e. evil heart).

Bitterness is the root of many problems. A bitter heart spawns all sorts of evil reactions. Wrath, anger, clamor, slander and malice are all means by which resentment expresses itself. Bitterness cannot stay in the heart by itself. It is true, bitterness can stay dormant for a long period until a storm arises, but it will come. Meanwhile, it slowly poisons the life of that relationship.[53]

We should discard all of these expressions of hatred and get rid of them completely. When a person wants to remove a tree, he does not just cut off the branches. He has to get down to the dirty work of digging out the roots. If the main roots are not eliminated, the branches will grow back stronger than before. The real solution is not just to get rid of the expression of anger but to deal with the root of bitterness from which hatred grows. Let us see how bitterness does its evil work even in normal people like you and me.

The reason bitterness is so devastating is that it provides the justification for being mean, cold, short-tempered or unpleasant to others. Bitterness nurtures itself through legitimizing itself. Most people know that it is wrong to hate others. Our conscience tells us that it is wrong to do evil to others. This limits the expression of our hatred towards others. If people are going to persist in their meanness toward someone, they need some way to override the guilt function of their conscience. Otherwise, the guilt would pile on so thick that they would have to cease being mean. They would begin to feel quite bad (guilty) about it.

Bitterness provides the needed short circuit that allows them to bypass the work of their consciences, not only to do evil to others but even to feel smug and self-righteous about it.

How does bitterness do this? Bitterness fools the person by tricking his conscience. The person only needs to dwell upon the way someone offended him, and he becomes free from the defensive action of his con-

---

[53] Please note that bitterness does this with all kinds of relationships. Why are teens so often in a rage against their parents? Look for resentment and bitterness. Resolving bitterness in all relationships is a must.

science. A biological parallel might be the effect of drugs or alcohol on a person's body. The nerve connections become dulled so that he is able, in a drunken stupor, to do things that he would never otherwise do. Bitterness is a soul drug. It allows people to do evil things that they would not otherwise think themselves capable of doing.

I remember a former neighbor. He had so much bitterness that it destroyed his marriage and his relationship with his children. He would ride around with a gun in his car in case he got enough nerve to kill himself. It is important to know how bitterness works. Although it is very powerful, it can, thanks to God's grace in Christ, be disabled.

Bitterness works as long as it is being focused on. One would think that a person would spit out the poisonous venom of bitterness from his life just as one might spit out a sour lemon. But people hold on to it. Why? The one who feels he or she has been wronged gains a slight sense of power and control. In most cases, these people are convinced that they are God's appointed people to carry out justice. This is the "nurture offense" stage in the above diagram.

Through self-pity they disable their conscience and allow the deadening effects of bitterness to continue, and even worsen. They believe that they are doing good when they are in fact doing evil. It is this faulty sense of justice that blinds them to the evil of their actions.

When this happens in a marriage, the spouse puts him or herself at complete odds against his mate. Nursing the hatred and pain extenuates the 'twoness' and virtually eliminates the 'oneness' of marriage. They are married, but they act as two. Two opponents. Bitterness makes this division permanent as long as he or she wants it to last. Let's take an even closer look at how bitterness works its wretched evil.

A Peek Inside of Bitterness

"See to it that no one comes short of the grace of God; that no root of bitterness springing up causes trouble, and by it many be defiled" (Hebrews 12:15).

The scriptures reveal many insights about bitterness. Hebrews 12:15 states three things. Each of them will be further discussed below.

- Short of God's grace (The mark of bitterness)
- Root of bitterness (The nature of bitterness)
- Being defiled   (The result of bitterness)

1) Short of God's grace (The mark of bitterness)

People can claim to belong to God and yet not have God's blessing upon their lives. This is also true with bitter people who profess to know Christ. Hebrews 12:15 says that some people come 'short of the grace of God.' Bitter people have withheld grace and therefore, grace and mercy are withheld from them. Jesus clearly stated this in the Sermon on the Mount while instructing others on how to pray and then immediately afterwards emphasized it.

For if you forgive men for their transgressions, your heavenly Father will also forgive you. But if you do not forgive men, then your Father will not forgive your transgressions. (Matthew 6:14-15)

Jesus talked a lot about forgiveness for it lies at the heart of the gospel. Jesus tells us of the man who refused to forgive a person who owed him a very little even when the king had already forgiven his much larger debt (see side bar). When we withhold grace, it will be withheld from us.

Those people who are caught in the net of bitterness think that they have the right to carry out their vindictive spirit. When in fact, Jesus clearly states that these people who refuse to forgive others are in great danger. We know these passages raise all sorts of questions about what does the phrase "comes short of the grace of God" mean. Does it mean that a Christian can lose his salvation? Jesus describes their judgment in a very vivid way. We will leave it as Jesus did. He reveals the high cost of having an unforgiving heart. The point is simple: no one has any right to carry bitterness in his soul. We must always forgive everyone, including our mate.

God's grace will be held back from us as long as we hold it back from another. An unforgiving spirit is like withdrawing life and allowing death to set into our bodies. No wonder bitter people have the saddest marriages and lives on earth. Will you right now settle in your heart, once for all, to always be quick to forgive others no matter how much the pain and rejection you feel? This is the way of Jesus.

The Importance of Forgiving One Another

Matthew 18:23-35 by Jesus

For this reason the kingdom of heaven may be compared to a certain king who wished to settle accounts with his slaves. And when he had begun to settle them, there was brought to him one who owed him ten thousand talents. But since he did not have the means to repay, his lord commanded him to be sold, along with his wife and children and all that he had, and repayment to be made. The slave therefore falling down, prostrated himself before him, saying, 'Have patience with me, and I will repay you everything.' And the lord of that slave felt compassion and released him and forgave him the debt. But that slave went out and found one of his fellow slaves who owed him a hundred denarii; and he seized him and began to choke him, saying, 'Pay back what you owe.'

So his fellow slave fell down and began to entreat him, saying, 'Have patience with me and I will repay you.' He was unwilling however, but went and threw him in prison until he should pay back what was owed. So when his fellow slaves saw what had happened, they were deeply grieved and came and reported to their lord all that had happened.

Then summoning him, his lord said to him, 'You wicked slave, I forgave you all that debt because you entreated me. Should you not also have had mercy on your fellow slave, even as I had mercy on you?'

And his lord, moved with anger, handed him over to the torturers until he should repay all that was owed him. So shall My heavenly Father also do to you, if each of you does not forgive his brother from your heart.

2) Root of bitterness (The nature of bitterness)

Hebrews 12:15 continues by mentioning the 'root of bitterness.' There are two aspects to this root.

First, the scripture speaks of the sure way bitterness can cling to our souls. A plant's resistance comes from its roots. If there are no roots, the plant is easily pulled up. But because the root is there, then the plant with its evident branches, leaves and blossoms will in time manifest itself. If a person is bitter or acts bitterly, then he should know that at some time in the past a seed of bitterness was allowed to grow within his soul.[54] Something has happened in his or her past that must be properly dealt with in order to eliminate the bitterness.

Second, we see that the root will spring forth all sorts of diabolical troubles. These I believe are the manifestations of bitterness along with their consequences (refer to the former tree diagram). The larger the manifestations of bitterness, the greater the root of bitterness has grown. Bitterness never brings about good results. Justice is never served. Grace is never given. Marriages are destroyed.

Third, we observe that some roots can be bigger and deeper than others. Nurturing the root of bitterness causes it to grow. If we want a better marriage, bitterness is not the route to go! A gracious spirit is the

---

[54] There is some question as to whether this seed came from the outside and was implanted in his heart or that the evil nature produced it, but the results and cure are the same. It is the evil nature that nourishes and encourages bitterness. We can find full forgiveness and peace of heart through Jesus Christ.

opposite of a bitter spirit (see diagram). Each time we justify (think it is okay) ourselves for resenting someone, we 'nurture' the root of bitterness. It grows. Instead, we must begin to confess that our bitter heart is wrong, for Jesus says it is wrong, and seek forgiveness. This whole bitter root system can be put to death.

3) Many be defiled (The result of bitterness)

The scripture passage above says in a authoritative word that people who are bitter will be defiled and that the defilement in most cases spreads over into the lives of others. This is clear. Can one spouse be bitter and the other not be influenced by it? Clamor speaks of raging words. Malice is the evil that is finally carried out. Anger is the means through which displeasure is expressed. Wrath is the volatile anger that erupts like a volcano. Bitterness springs forth all sorts of trouble. And to make things worse, those who are the victims of such acts, often become bitter themselves.

Instead of being a person God uses to extend His grace and mercy to others, this person has become an instrument through which Satan carries out his diabolical work. Anyone who plays in the mud gets muddy. Those who play with muddy people get muddied. Anyone who plays in the field of hatred and scorn will be defiled. One reason divorce is so horrible is the bitterness that defiles not only the spouse but their children and friends. So many acidic words are used. This pain is clearly documented both in research and more importantly in the lives around those who allow bitterness to reside in their hearts.

Summary

Let's think about these things from the perspective of marriage. People get married to have a loving relationship and all the good fruits that come from such a relationship. When bitterness implants itself in either of the spouses' heart, they end up with terrible troubles. The problems might first be observable by one's disappointment over no longer having a warm and loving relationship. The difficulties can, however, become so overwhelming that life together becomes intolerable.

The seed (the offense) must first be planted. Roots will then grow. If we allow the seed to sprout and take root, then the plant of bitterness will grow and increasingly denigrate other areas of our lives and those around us.

On the other hand, we can pull that root out. If we just ignore the minor offenses, we end up allowing the seed to remain. In such cases, we will forget that the seed was ever planted and be unaware that it is still buried in the ground with a slowly growing root. By God's grace we need to dig the dirt away from the root to expose it. This is done by acknowledging how you have opposed the Lord's way of love and forgiveness. Be specific about the words you have said, the actions you have taken, and the attitudes you have held. Once the dirt is pulled back, then the root can easily be pulled out. Let's go on and see how to do this. Meanwhile, don't let the bitter seed be planted in the first place! Avoid taking offense by always consciously forgiving one another. "Love covers a multitude of sins" (1 Peter 4:8).

Life Application: Is it a policy in your marriage to always quickly forgive each other?

B) Principles for Overcoming Bitterness

As we begin discussing how to eliminate bitterness, we need to see how roots become entrenched in the soil. Many people have attempted to pull out the roots to no avail. As a home gardener, I know how difficult it is to pull out weeds that have been allowed to grow. Let's look at some of the main principles we have learned.

The bitter root grows from a seed. The seed is the original offense. The offense is an event, a word, a comment, a facial expression or some such thing that has been perceived as a wrong done to me that I never forgave. Until this issue is identified, it cannot be completely pulled out. It can be made smaller by ripping the plant apart. I might even get part of the root, but it will continue growing unless it is completely eradicated. One of the hardest parts of identifying this offending event is the exposure of our hearts to the pain we felt at that time. We need to again face this pain and disappointment so that we can properly respond to it this time.

The 'stuff' between a husband and wife create distance between them ('twoness') rather than oneness.

• The strength of the root is dependent upon how much the bitterness has been nurtured. The bitterness is nurtured by taking secret delight in plotting revenge. The root of bitterness is protected by a faulty defense logic that asserts my right or duty to harm another. As long as these both stand, then the root cannot be extracted. These faulty arguments must be exposed in order to get at the root. By exposing and destroying this line of thinking, God can start speaking again to my conscience through guilt. That in turn begins to restore me to normality. As long as bitterness is lodged in the heart, pride in obtaining a "righteous" judgment will keep guilt from doing its needed job in my life.

• Bitter people are difficult to counsel because they continually go through a cycle of thoughts that both justify themselves and accuse the other. Usually breakthroughs do not come until the cycle is broken. Before deep root extraction begins, we need to discern how Satan confuses one's cycle of thoughts. It is much like a rut. As we go around in the cycle, it gets harder and harder to respond any differently. Even if I am able to get out for a moment, it is very easy to fall back in.

• God's Word must penetrate my mind so that I can see that Jesus really condemns what I am doing. Being bitter is always wrong. Taking God's vengeance into my own hands is also wrong. I must recognize that there are dire consequences to my marriage, family and relationships if I do not change. Think about whether you now have a troubled marriage. Troubles are one tool that God uses to cause a person to be open to the truth and then be delivered from the deception. He shows us how bad it is to be bitter. He wants us to connect the bad consequence with our decision to tolerate bitterness.

The difficulty in pulling out the root is that it is so intertwined that it is hard to isolate and identify let alone pull out. Usually God will use a crisis to sufficiently humble me to the point that I am willing to deal with bitterness the way God desires. When I am willing to forgive, then the whole root of bitterness is exposed and begins to wither. Once I forgive, God forgives me. Let's go through some basic concepts that are necessary to heal a bitter heart and how they relate to a marriage.

1) Jesus said that we are to forgive with liberality.

Then Peter came and said to Him, "Lord, how often shall my brother sin against me and I forgive him? Up to seven times?" Jesus said to him, "I do not say to you, up to seven times, but up to seventy times seven." (Matthew 18:21-22).

We are to forgive everyone all the time. Just preceding the story above about the man who did not forgive, Jesus said these words.

Because of people's weaknesses, people often try to find circumstances which excuse them from having to forgive another. There are not any! God's command to bring forgiveness to every possible offense swallows up every opportunity for bitterness to sneak in. I go by this policy. I liberally treat people with love. If this general love is not sufficient, then I need to take another step. I purposely forgive that person in my heart. We will talk about how to do this later. As ambassadors of His kingdom, we have the right to distribute God's mercy and love to the people of the world.

Namely, that God was in Christ reconciling the world to Himself, not counting their trespasses against them, and He has committed to us the word of reconciliation. Therefore, we are ambassadors for Christ ... (2 Corinthians 5:19-20).

Forgiveness does not mean someone has not done something wrong. It usually means they did! The difference is that you are, as Jesus instructed, not holding that moral debt against them. We forgive because God forgave us. By forgiving another, you allow God's divine grace to mightily work through your life just as Jesus did. It is only here we find real hope to overcome severe bitterness and resentment problems in marriages.

Marriage: The husband and wife must continually forgive each other for every wrong that is done or perceived to have been done. There must not be even one situation or circumstance that the spouse will not forgive. When getting married, it is wise to realize that your spouse, no matter how much you sense their love at that moment, will one day say or do some offensive things. Make a decision that no matter how mean, harsh or selfish your spouse might be, you will forgive him or her because Christ has forgiven you for much worse things. Take steps to clean out the issues from the past that have not been forgiven.

Presently forgive anything that needs to be forgiven. Prepare for the future by pledging to God that you will forgive everyone, every time, for everything.

2) The scriptures state that taking vengeance is God's prerogative alone.

Never take your own revenge, beloved, but leave room for the wrath of God, for it is written, "VENGEANCE IS MINE, I WILL REPAY," says the Lord. (Romans 12:19)

When man attempts to distribute justice, it only produces further offenses. Personal vengeance is a far cry from God's judgment. God tells us to release those who offend us. God Himself will carry out proper justice. He is the just Judge who will exercise full judgment when He sees fit. I have no right to 'pay back' a person for the wrong he has done to me. "Never pay back evil for evil to anyone" (Romans 12:17). We are not stating that man does not deserve judgment but only that we are not here on earth to carry out the job. Instead, we now have an obligation to love others and show people God's grace. We must focus on the job at hand. Indeed it is far more glorious!

Marriage: We are one in marriage. If we judge our spouse, then we make our spouse our enemy. Our spouse at times does deserve God's judgment. This is true. But judgment means that the time of grace has expired. Instead, we are to plead with God that He would give grace to our partner. I, as the spouse, am the most appropriate person to plead for God's grace on behalf of my partner. A forgiving spirit will protect our privilege of praying for another. Vengeance is not the way. Jesus refused to take revenge; so should we (cf. John 3:17).

3) God has told us to put on kindness, forgiveness and love and put off hatred and slander in all of its forms.

And so, as those who have been chosen of God, holy and beloved, put on a heart of compassion, kindness, humility, gentleness and patience; bearing with one another, and forgiving each other, whoever has a complaint against anyone; just as the Lord forgave you, so also should you. (Colossians 3:12-13).

But now you also, put them all aside: anger, wrath, malice, slander, and abusive speech from your mouth. (Colossians 3:8).

We must never embrace hatred even for a moment. We are God's people born of grace. These responses do not characterize Christ in us. Christ is working through us. We focus on extending grace. We are to forgive as we have been forgiven.

Marriage: Marriage gives us plenty of opportunities to show God's loving grace! We no doubt get offended more at home than anywhere else. Marriage is the place we are trained to be like our Father in heaven. Early each day we meet with our Lord asking for all the love and kindness that we need for all the people we will meet that day, including our spouse. Then we get to distribute His love throughout the day!

4) We must trust God even in difficult times of oppression.

Blessed are those who have been persecuted for the sake of righteousness, for theirs is the kingdom of heaven. Blessed are you when men cast insults at you, and persecute you, and say all kinds of evil against you falsely, on account of Me. Rejoice, and be glad, for your reward in heaven is great, for so they persecuted the prophets who were before you (Matthew 5:10-12).

We are sometimes tempted to alter our policies toward others when they mistreat us. The fact is that we are expected and commanded by God to love others at all times. We all owe each other love. When it is withheld through a mean and bitter heart, then God will in His time carry out judgment. Christ, however, gives us a totally different way from the world to think about oppression. He tells us that it is a circumstance to take joy in. We can turn the evil one's purpose around by loving those who hate us.

We can turn the occasion for bitterness into an opportunity to minister. Instead of holding back God's grace by being bitter, we deliberately forgive and receive God's grace to love that person. This is the strongest weapon we have in breaking the hardness of our spouse. Romans 12:20-21 speaks about allowing the conscience to work fully when we respond with loving reactions rather than bitterness.

> *But if your enemy is hungry, feed him, and if he is thirsty, give him a drink; for in so doing you will heap burning coals upon his head. Do not be overcome by evil, but overcome evil with good. (Romans 12:20-21).*

Marriage: Even when our spouse turns on us with a mean enemy-like spirit, God has given us a clear plan of operation.

1) First, I am to forgive. Only by forgiving can I take the next step.

2) I am then to treat my spouse with a love that they really do not deserve. If a husband loses his temper with his wife, we all know that the husband does not 'deserve' any kindness in return. But it is through extending undeserved kindness (perhaps making a very nice meal) that we have our only chance of turning around a mean spouse.

3) I am to rejoice in my opportunity to show love in very difficult situations. Why? Because everyone who witnesses love in such extenuating circumstances knows it is from God. It is a modern day miracle occurring in our living rooms or bedrooms.

The truth of God provides the weapons we need to destroy the greatest ploys of the enemy. Bitterness is no exception. Deep roots of bitterness are been pulled out of people's lives by God's truth. These people are not the same any more. Satan had dominated their minds with bitterness, but now they are set free by God's powerful truths mentioned above.

Although we know these truths, we need work through the steps of destroying the root of bitterness. We have the ammunition. Now we need to apply it to our lives.

C) Steps to Eliminate a Bitter Heart

The following thoughts are good for keeping bitterness away from our lives as well as for laying the foundation to take down the stronghold of bitterness. Do you see how we are destroying the root of bitterness? Step by step we apply God's Word to the faulty thinking behind the bitterness. As we carefully inject God's truth into the conscience, people are further convicted by God's Spirit. Yes, they might still be prideful, but if we are praying, we should see that God is opening a door for reconciliation.

We will be addressing this issue with a couple in mind. Let us consider two situations: 1) A mild case of bitterness and 2) A more extreme case of bitterness.

1) Mild case of bitterness

First, remember that the seed of bitterness has already been planted and has started to put down roots. We are not saying that great danger is not in store for this couple. The fact is that if they do not pull out its tiny root, then it can easily grow to be a strong tree. This is what Hebrews 12:15 warns us of. We should also remember that as much as we accept bitterness, then we are to the same degree not able to carry out love. The marriage will very quickly decline in affection and warmth.

The only advantage is that this person's mind is not totally blocked by certain lies so he can still reason. In other words, the couple can still have a normal conversation. The cycle of lies only infiltrates part of the mind.

In this case, we need to find the seed of bitterness. Name the little offense that caused a reaction. Offense can happen so easily. Even if we think we are innocent of any wrong doing, bitterness can still grow in our partner. Bitterness can sometimes be founded upon an assumed wrong motive. I assumed that he did a certain thing because... when in fact his motivation was flawless. So we must always act as an off duty policeman.

When we notice our spouse's coldness, then we need to discern what is going on. We need to thoroughly pull that seed out before it puts down any roots. Once the roots are in place, it is more difficult to remove them. If we do not take care of it as quickly as possible, it allows our spouse to feel that coldness or highly charged emotions are the best way to let us know that they are offended. Be careful. As soon as the seed of bitterness is implanted, it begins to sends out its roots.

What do I do when I sense my spouse is giving me the "cold shoulder" and isolates me?

Check for something you have done wrong

First, pray and ask the Lord to prompt you about anything you have done wrong. Pay close attention to what He brings to your mind. Then you can gently ask your spouse what you have done to offend him or her. I would like to think the latter works, but more often than not, my pride is too big for me to be corrected. In other words, I probably would have not have caused the offense if I was sensitive to the Lord in the first place. But due to the urgency of preventing this problem from turning into bitterness, I still try to resolve it right away.

Resolve to solve it before sleep

BE ANGRY, AND yet DO NOT SIN; do not let the sun go down on your anger, and do not give the devil an opportunity (Ephesians 4:26-27).

The scriptures are quite clear. Anger, which is a normal and good emotion, can be turned into bitterness if it is not dealt with quickly. I am not to let the sun go down on my anger. I am to deal with any anger that very day. Anger's purpose is to motivate me to deal with something quickly. But if I delay solving the problem by confronting the person, bitterness takes root. Then the anger that urged me to a timely resolution actually becomes a weapon against me. I might use that anger and wrath to hurl words that are laced with fire that further wound my partner.

My wife and I go to bed at close to the same time. We have some of our best conversations in bed before falling asleep. We can easily detect if the normal tender kindness is missing. It might be cold back treatment or brusque words in response to the other's question. Sometimes we sense that something is not quite right. If both husband and wife are determined to solve matters before we sleep, then we have a good solid platform for reconciliation. I can remember praying late into the night on several occasions for God to heal our relationship.

God suggests that by allowing the offense to brew overnight, roots of bitterness already begin to grow. What amazing growth! We give the devil an opportunity to toy with our minds when we have sinned. Sin shuts off our sensitivity to God and His truth. As long as this sin is not resolved, then we give an opening to Satan. He can deviously move in with his temptations and set up a base through which he can destroy our marriage.

Forgive and do not wait to be asked

Do not wait for your spouse to ask for forgiveness. Just forgive him or her. Not a few individuals have asked me whether they should forgive someone who has not asked for forgiveness. Jesus says we need to. It is much nicer and the process more complete if the offender asks, but even if he hasn't, we still must forgive.

Many Christians have allowed an offense to stay in their heart too long. Every time this is done, our relationship with that person sours. So if our spouse has not lived out the law of love, then we should simply

dismiss it. If we cannot, then we should go through the process of confrontation, apology and forgiveness.

Even if our spouse does not ask for forgiveness, we should still forgive them in our hearts. We do not need to tell them, "I forgive you"
since that can sound rather arrogant. We should, however, tell our Lord
we have forgiven him. As we do it in our hearts, we should seek a way to
concretely express our love to our spouse. We can always seal our forgiveness with a prayer for blessing on that person.

"How can I forgive someone that doesn't ask for forgiveness?"
Forgiveness is a technical term. Perhaps we can better understand it in
the context of a money debt. If someone owes you ten dollars, then he is
morally obligated to pay you back. However, if you choose to, you can
forgive the debt. That person will owe you nothing. The account is settled regarding that $10. What did you do to forgive? You chose to bear
the debt yourself and release the debtor from his obligation to repay
you. In most cases you would state that you would not demand a pay-
ment. You forgave the debt.

The same thing happens when I forgive a spiritual debt. A husband
should not have spoken roughly when driving, but he snapped at his
wife. The spiritual law of love has been broken. He owes her. (He actually owes her kindness).

It might take ten hours for the Spirit of God to work on his heart.
Should she nurture the offense the whole time? Absolutely not! Otherwise she will have a poor response and sin herself. She is commanded to
forgive.

Instead she should simply say in heart to God that she forgives the
spiritual debt her husband has incurred. She chooses to bear the debt
herself and release him from his obligation. Then the spiritual debt is
gone just like the $10. The account is clear. Her heart is free to express
her love for him.

God might decide to chasten our spouse, but that is His responsibility. Even though we forgave the debt, he still is responsible before God for his sin. This is why we need to make two apologies when we sin against a person, first to God and then to that person.

As a Christian matures, he will naturally (really supernaturally) forgive those around him all the time. It will becomes more of an unconscious spiritual discipline. Instead of focusing on what people owe him, he will remember how much he owes Christ who forgave him of such a great debt.

Gently confront

This is difficult to implement until the couple is aware of the seriousness of the problem. The offender has in most cases done wrong and is on the defensive. The offended is thinking he is right to be offended. So who should bring up the issue? Whoever notices the problem first. Much like cancer, the earlier it is detected, the easier it is to deal with.

More than likely the offended spouse will not bring up the issue. We need to be so careful when confronting. Prayer and humility go a long way in helping the process along. Never start by saying, "You did ..." If you are the offended, begin by saying,

"When you said those words about eating this afternoon, it really hurt me. I tried to put it out of my mind, but it really bothers me." If you are the offender and notice that your spouse is keeping his or her distance, bring up the issue with something like, "I know I spoke roughly this afternoon, could we talk about it a little. Let me start by apologizing for the way I spoke. ..."

We do not want to wait too long trying to straighten out the relationship. Details may be forgotten. Other things may distract you. Neither should we react immediately to the situation for then we would tend to be defensive. The words 'speak the truth in love' are very important here. We should also remember to confront in such a way that we are not accusing the other but rather encouraging conversation about the situation. Be ready to forgive where we have done wrong.

If I see that my wife is giving me the cool or silent treatment, more likely than not, I have somehow offended her. I might know what the offending incident or attitude is or I might not. Sometimes I think I know what it is but realize she has misjudged me. It does not really matter much. I could be wrong. I will not be defensive. If I am found in the wrong, then I will apologize. The relationship is most important. My pride must go. I can follow through by asking her, "Is something wrong?" Perhaps I could say, "I noticed that you are quiet. Did I do anything that hurt you?" A wife might say, "You haven't been talking much lately. Have I somehow displeased you?"

In any case, we must be dedicated to caring for and preserving the oneness of our relationship.

Kindly discuss

We need to foster positive conversation, talk about what we think we did and get down to discussing what we really did. We must be careful not to accuse each other. A person might wonder if it is worth talking about it. "Isn't it better just to forget about it?" If our spouse is offended, then we need to deal with it.

If a couple regularly argues, then there is probably a lot of resentment already stored in the heart from other unresolved issues. Conflict arises easily in such situations. Refuse to accuse. Be a true friend. You are not trying to make yourself look right but have peace with each other.

Give both sides time to adequately present their own understanding of the issue. Remember, you are looking for the 'thorn' that has caused offense. If spotted, then you can go on to the next step.

Give time

Let's not corner our spouse. God's Spirit convicts us of sin. We do not need to take over His job. We merely bring up the issue so that it does not sprout and slowly grow further. Again, we need to talk as much as possible and then pray. When a person starts getting defensive, then either change the direction of your conversation or come back and talk more later (hopefully the same day!) At times after we have fully discussed the issues, I have suggested, "Don't you think you should apologize?" She positively responded to this timely call.

Confess and forgive

When a person has done or said something wrong, he or she should apologize by first stating what he has done wrong and then ask for forgiveness. For example: "I'm sorry for speaking so rudely to you at lunch. It was improper. Will you please forgive me?" Of course we need to ask the Lord to forgive us too. If both partners have done wrong, let the husband go first. If one spouse is stubborn, then let the humble one start.

What happens if only one spouse apologizes when both have done wrong? We are so foolishly stubborn at times. Go as far as you can. Let the person who did apologize first rejoice God has cleared that part up. His or her heart is clean. Now he can start praying for the spouse. Be warned, though, that your spouse may accuse you of manipulation when you start to pray.

The one that has been forgiven needs to be careful or he could be offended by his spouse's unwillingness to apologize. He could end up worse than at the start. If we act according to the policy that we are going to forgive, even if the other person does not forgive, then Satan cannot sneak in and take advantage of our progress. You are going to forgive their debt of love even if he does not ask for it.

Now if the stubborn spouse asks for forgiveness later on, forgive and affirm your love for one another. And praise God that no root of bitterness grew up out of that situation.

2) Handling Extreme Bitterness

What we have just said about dealing with mild bitterness is also true in dealing with extreme bitterness. There are other things, however, that also need attention. Bitterness is not as easy to remove when its roots have grown deep over the years. The best approach is to start dealing with offenses as they come up.

Always focus on our hope that God is with us

Always have hope in what God can do. We should not say that any situation is impossible. I have seen two absolute miracles in the way God dealt with people bound by bitterness. One was about to be shipped to a long-term psychiatric unit. The other person would have been there had others known what he was thinking. Their pride was sky high. But God intervened through many people's prayers. His abounding grace melted that mountain of pride down to nothing within minutes. Always have hope. Always press the Lord for deliverance. Today is the day of salvation.

Remember that the evil one does not want anyone to intercede for these people. This is why grace and mercy are the only things that can break through such barriers. If you are offended by them, then you will not pray for them. We need to be in the ministry mode. Think of yourself as one light in the very dark world of the embittered spouse. At times you (as an outsider) might be the only light in a very dark cave where both spouses are bitterly angry at each other.

Expect trouble: Deeply entrenched roots

We have explained that there are two faulty perceptions: (1) A focus on the offense and offender, and (2) justification of one's wrong response. They grow in parallel. We need to take the different truths mentioned above and share them with our spouse as much as possible. They might spit it out like a baby who rejects a new kind of food. We need to seek God's timing.

Sometimes, if we can identify the real offense, it can be of great help. They might be generally mad at you but not know why.

At other times it helps to show the terrible consequences that God has brought upon them because of their disobedience. We must also remind them that in disobedience to God they have not forgiven someone. Go beyond this and remind them of the many acts of kindness that they have missed because of the hatred in their heart.

That is right. Mention the truth so that their pile of guilt will overflow their defensive system of self-justification. Again, remember we are not doing this in an accusing way but in a gentle and yet explanatory way. We are just uncovering what is there. We do not need to accuse. By simply exposing it, we let the Spirit of God do His work.

Look for miraculous breakthroughs

We need to live out our lives as Jesus did in Isaiah 50.

> "The Lord God has given Me the tongue of disciples, that I may know how to sustain the weary one with a word. He awakens Me morning by morning, He awakens My ear to listen as a disciple. The Lord God has opened My ear; and I was not disobedient, nor did turn back." (Isaiah 50:4-5).

Intimidating foes can only be broken by waiting upon the Lord. The counselor or friend must throw himself on the Lord for grace and truth. He needs God's grace to be gracious to a mean and bitter person. This is not easy.

He needs the truth that God gives him. Notice how in the passage above that he was a listener. He was a disciple learning from the Father. This is what Jesus regularly did in the course of His ministry. There is no greater spouse than the one who intercedes like this on behalf of his or her spouse.

Make sure they know and hear the gospel

Those who do not exercise grace perhaps have never been saved. They might profess to be a Christian, but we should have them tell us again how they came to know the Lord. If we have experienced God's grace, then we are less likely to be engrossed in taking revenge. Make sure they hear the Gospel of Christ Jesus that God died for sinners. I like to share from Romans 5:1-10 where we see three ways we are described before we are saved: helpless (6), ungodly (6) and sinners (8). All grace. We deserved the worse but received the best.

Be patient

The process might take a while. They might even be bitter toward you. Think of it like this. Though it might not sound encouraging, they might not acknowledge their bitterness until the very end of their lives. We have seen several people come to the Lord on their deathbed. But even if it takes so long, are you not prepared to so love your spouse? We hope so. This is the marriage covenant we have made before the Lord. It is also the New Covenant principles of love and forgiveness.

Distract with the truth

We know that bitterness grows and sustains itself by focusing on the offense of the other. Pray for wisdom on how to take their mind off such topics. Sometimes pain will do it. Other times getting them away from their environment. Often they are not eager to meet new people. But with these opportunities to change their circumstances, try to share some illustrations of the power of forgiveness. Start by sharing your story and how God saved you!

If you can lead them away from thinking in the same pattern, then you can implant the seed of truth that can combat the seed of bitterness. For example, we might interweave the truth about how only God has the right to judge others. Oh, how we need to pray for such people caught in Satan's snare!

Ask questions

We can ask them key questions: Why do you seem so unhappy? Why don't you want to go anywhere? Were you always like this? What started your bitterness? If people have such bitterness, they sometimes will tell you what is wrong but be very biased. We need to explore for the truth. Ask them if they are willing to take a few steps to regain that beautiful marriage.

D) Practical steps for the couple to take

We would like each couple to take a few important steps. Each spouse that is reading this should understand that bitterness is always wrong and never beneficial. It is a root that springs forth trouble. None of us want marriages like that. Would you make a few decisions today?

Always forgive your spouse. You will always forgive everyone. If you have other thoughts that tell you that you must be mean to him or her, then just note that these are satanic temptations. Reject them. The Lord's voice is calling us to be kind and gracious as He is always gracious to you.

Substitute your name in the following line of commitment,

"I _____ (your name) will always forgive my spouse right away for any wrong thing he or she does against me." Remember by your forgiveness you are not stating that your spouse deserves forgiveness or that his or her evil is unimportant, but simply that you forgive the moral debt your mate owes you.

Catch up on the past. You want to remove the entire bitter root out of your own heart. It is true that you cannot do this for your spouse, but you can at least clear up what bitterness lies in your own heart. If you are a couple doing this, then each of you should take a piece of paper and write down everything your spouse has done that has bothered you. If you have forgotten it, then it was covered in your general love. Focus only on those things that bother you, and about which you feel a little bit of resentment over. If a couple is doing this together, then let the husband start.

He should lead in a prayer in which they seek His forgiveness as a couple for all of their stored up bitterness. After this, the wife should confirm this in prayer. Then the husband should go through his list. He should not attack her or discuss any of the issues. His wife might want to discuss them later. Now is time for forgiveness. The husband might want to start with the most offending items. He should name them one by one and then tell his spouse that although he has been offended by these things, he now wholly forgives every one of them.

He then needs to ask her for forgiveness for storing up resentment and withholding his love and grace. He can say, "I have sinned by storing up resentment and withholding my full love and affection from you. Will you forgive me for all of this?" The wife should follow. After doing this, I would suggest going back to the Lord and asking His help in making you a couple full of His mercy and grace, always ready to forgive.

Your spouse might not be here today. That is fine. You still have follow-up work. It might be a bit more awkward, but it is still needed. If your spouse is a Christian, then share what you have learned and what you would like to do. Even if your spouse does not have an understanding or agree in heart about these matters, you can still proceed.

First confess your sins to the Lord.

Write your list and confess them. Because of your resentment you have failed your spouse. In your heart (this is the big difference) forgive them.

Aloud ask forgiveness for your failures.

Remember, it is not necessary to tell your spouse that you were offended or by what you were offended if you can just simply forgive them. This is more for you than for him or her. But at least tell the Lord. If your spouse is a non-Christian or easily irritated, do not mention this process. They might take it to mean that you are attacking them. The list is so that you can fully clean out your register of bitterness. Afterwards, burn up or rip up your list. Discard it. It is gone. Now express your love. Hopefully, your spouse will notice the change in you and ask you about it.That is the time to share God's work in your life.

Discuss procedure. You have made a commitment not to withhold forgiveness. If you have done this with your spouse, then you can set up some clear rules that will help you resolve differences.

(1) Urgency of forgiveness (by bed time).

(2) Arrange a specific signal that you need to talk. (e.g. Put a certain empty vase on the dining room table, a blue cloth on your spouse's pillow, etc.).

(3) Arrange for a certain place for discussion (e.g. dining room table).

(4) Peaceably mention your resentment.

(5) Pray together before beginning any discussion.

Conclusion

A single well-placed stone brought down the towering Goliath. In marriages that little stone is a forgiving spirit. When a person affirms release of that moral debt as Jesus commanded, he then opens the streams of God's grace to shower upon him and his relationships with others. Instead of playing into the devil's hand, the spouse becomes God's divine agent of love. A forgiving spirit releases all the hostilities one has stored in his heart. A forgiving spirit again allows God's love to touch you and your spouse with His sweet waters of grace. No offense is so great or enduring that it cannot or should not be forgiven.

There is pain in forgiveness. Sometimes the pain is severe. But still the words and example of Jesus call us to trust Him as we faithfully obey Him in always forgiving everyone. Let the spirit of forgiveness rule our homes and hearts, and our marriages and families will never be the same.

Jesus will live there! Jesus' command to liberally forgive is not to limit us to some lesser life but to free us to live in the power of His Spirit. Our ministry is to bring grace into our marriage not to cause a shortage of it. With this resentment gone, the marriage is instantly so much sweeter and pleasant. Is this not the reason we got married in the first place?

Chapter #7 Study Questions

1. What happens when bitterness settles into a marriage?

2. What are the 'brothers and cousins' of bitterness? See Ephesians 4:31.

3. Why isn't it sufficient just to stop doing and saying bad things to our spouse?

4. Explain the way bitterness grows (the bitterness cycle).

5. Can a person receive God's grace when he has bitterness in his heart? Explain.

6. Explain one truth from the phrase 'root of bitterness.'

7. The seed of bitterness is the offense in your heart. How does it grow into a root?

8. How does Jesus' teaching on forgiveness tell us how to solve problems with bitterness?

9. What does the teaching of vengeance have to do with helping people do away with bitterness?

10. How does Romans 12:20-21 reveal to us a special key to avoid being offended?

11. Why does the teaching, 'do not let the sun go down on your anger' help us avoid bitterness?

12. How can we forgive even if the other person does not ask us to?

13. Reflect on your own response to people who offend you. How do you tend to respond?

14. Have you made the commitment per order of Jesus Christ to always quickly forgive everyone, including your spouse? Choose to be a vehicle of God's grace.

Section #3: Friendship

Chapters #8-10

Creating a Great Marriage!

Building a
Great Marriage

#8 Cultivating Intimacy in Marriage

Every wedding is the fulfillment of many hopes and dreams. Maybe you can remember back to when you were readying yourself for your marriage. I remember writing love poems. Linda, on the other hand, would make matching outfits. We were probably like most couples, which have their heads far above the clouds. Each couple is convinced that their own marriage will be different from those that face problems. God has so wired each couple to wish and dream for the best. Why?

A common life, a shared heart.

We are not sure of all the reasons for this, but it does seem that the Lord reveals two significant things to the couple through the brief period of engagement:

1.   The true longings of the heart: A true honest, endearing and faithful relationship that brings a greater joy, love and sense of fulfillment.

2.   The depth of commitment: An unselfishness and exclusive devotion to love only one another.

God in His grace grants each couple a foretaste of how great their marriage really could be. He gives them something to aspire to. Married couples typically are caught off guard shortly after the wedding. The reality of selfishness sets in. If the couple allows, bitterness will settle into the couple's relationship right to the grave. Couples cannot go much further than tolerating the selfishness of their spouse without God's plan and power built into their lives through Jesus Christ.

God pronounces each couple 'one' on their wedding day. Are they one? Yes. But there still remains the need for the couple to grow into it every day of their married lives. Married life serves as a constant opportunity for each spouse to live out what deep down they know they should be doing. As a married couple lives together, they will have many opportunities to eliminate those apparent fissures between them and become one. Married life in summary, then, is an opportunity to grow in intimacy. In this chapter you will learn how to cultivate deeper intimacy in your marriage.

A) Understanding Intimacy

Through your previous reading, you have seen two main ways to obtain a great marriage. First, you have come to understand what biblical marriage looks like. You have acquired God's view of marriage. As long as you look at marriage from man's point of view, distorted perspectives will kill all valiant attempts to have a great marriage. Marriage is not a man-made arrangement. It is God's design. We need to keep His design clearly in focus.

Second, you have seen how to recover from major setbacks in your marriage. As sinners you have, to different degrees, done harm to your marriage relationship. Fortunately, through Christ you can identify and resolve these problems. No matter how bad the past has been, by rightly approaching the problems, you can make significant changes for the better. Crises are opportunities designed by God to deepen your intimacy with your spouse and Him. Learning how to resolve conflicts brings you closer to one another.

In this third and last section the most delightful topic of how to gain a great marriage is discussed. If we needed to summarize the purpose of marriage in one word, it would be 'intimacy.' Many people are searching for greater intimacy in marriage. Marriage is designed to go beyond mere friendship.

What is Intimacy?

The concept of marital intimacy is derived from the Biblical principle of oneness. Although the word 'intimacy' is not used in the Bible, the concept is found there.

(1) First, the phrase 'the two shall become one' is used to define the marriage relationship. Intimacy is living in full view of the other so that the two function as one. God designed and appointed the husband to be head and for the wife to submit to the husband. If they are to function as one rather than two, then they need a way to relate to one another that does not cause conflict but encourages harmony.

The meaning of 'oneness' can be further understood by the words used to describe physical intimacy or sexual union. Our culture attempts to persuade us that the sexual experiences of animals and humans are the same. They are totally mistaken. Much more is at stake. The couple deep down knows that there is more to intimacy than sex but does not know how to attain it. Why else would a couple get married?

(2) Second, the Hebrew word used to describe the sexual relationship gives us a clue to what is missing. That word is 'to know.' The Hebrew word *yadah* has many usages including: to know, learn to know; perceive; find out and discern; discriminate, distinguish; know by experience; recognize, admit, acknowledge, confess; and have sexual union.

Now the man had relations (literally 'knew') with his wife Eve, and she conceived and gave birth to Cain, and she said, "I have gotten a manchild with the help of the LORD (Genesis 4:1).

When it says, for example, that Adam knew Eve, the scriptures are saying that they came together in sexual union. However, there is much more happening than the fulfillment of the individual's sexual drive. There is the intimate sharing of soul and person. Animals do not have souls or self-awareness. People do.

The married couple, then, is not just revealing their bodies to each other but their hearts as well. If a couple wants true intimacy, they need to deepen their relationship with each other. They need to 'know' each other in their different spheres of life. Although this might sound antiquated, just think, isn't this what the time before marriage is like?

I remember riding my bicycle three miles across our city in the dead of winter, in the snow and rain, to have a chance to talk to and spend time with my wonderful Linda. I would still do it. I still want to 'know' her more.

(3) Third, we can also see how intimacy is portrayed throughout the Bible. Many theologians have argued over the true meaning of The Song of Solomon. If you have not yet read this book, you should. The book

describes how a couple is romantically involved in each other's lives. You will also find some very interesting romantic poetry.

How beautiful you are, my darling, How beautiful you are! Your eyes are like doves behind your veil; Your hair is like a flock of goats That have descended from Mount Gilead. Your teeth are like a flock of newly shorn ewes Which have come up from their washing, All of which bear twins, And not one among them has lost her young. Your lips are like a scarlet thread, And your mouth is lovely. Your temples are like a slice of a pomegranate Behind your veil (Song of Solomon 4:1-3).

The Song of Solomon continues recording their wedding, their honeymoon and life after marriage. Some theologians could not accept such vivid sensual language. Instead of granting the Holy Scriptures the power to shape their views on marital relationships, they sought to veil the sensual, intimate language with a "spiritual only" interpretation. We do not need to shun this vivid picture of marital intimacy.

This book helps us understand the intimacy God desires with His people and affirms a healthy picture of an intimate marriage. The love between God and His people and a husband and wife share a number of similarities. Again, we must go beyond the shallow thinking that intimacy has only to do with sexual expression. Intimacy is all about having and growing deep relationships within covenant bounds.

Jesus shares more about this spiritual relationship that He desires with His people. He is not talking about sex. He is, however, speaking of an intimate relationship.

Abide in Me, and I in you. As the branch cannot bear fruit of itself, unless it abides in the vine, so neither can you, unless you abide in Me. I am the vine, you are the branches; he who abides in Me, and I in him, he bears much fruit; for apart from Me you can do nothing (John 15:4-5).

As we get lost in the identity and purpose of the Savior, He will blend with us and that relationship will produce much fruit. The fruit or works that are produced are a beautiful testimony of Christ living in a Christian. Can we see how the two parallel each other? Both are important and true. This is the mystery that the apostle speaks about.

> *For this cause a man shall leave his father and mother, and shall cleave to his wife; and the two shall become one flesh. This mystery is great; but I am speaking with reference to Christ and the church (Ephesians 5:31-32).*

(4)Fourth, let us note some clear commands in the Bible that have to do with intimacy between a husband and his wife. These four perspectives help shape the understanding that one spouse should have toward another. Watch out. You might be surprised!

Four Practical Perspectives of Marriage

1) Possession

> *But because of immoralities, let each man have his own wife, and let each woman have her own husband (1 Cor 7:2).*

The husband has his wife, and the wife has her husband. They belong to each other. They possess each other. Each is owned by the other. (This is the simple meaning of the Greek word to have or own.) s

2) Obligation

> *Let the husband fulfill his duty to his wife, and likewise also the wife to her husband (1 Cor 7:3).*

Husband and wife have certain obligations to fulfill toward each other. In this case he is speaking of sexual relations. Neither of them have a right to refuse their spouse. Their wills are constrained by their marriage covenant relationship. They have given up their right to do what they feel like.

3) Control

The wife does not have authority over her own body, but the husband does;
and likewise also the husband does not have authority over his own body, but
the wife does (1 Cor 7:4).

The husband and wife have surrendered to the wishes of their mates. Their wills and selves yield to the preference of each other. One's own will is lost in serving the other.

4) Devotion

But one who is married is concerned about the things of the world, how he
may please his wife, …but one who is married is concerned about the things
of the world, how she may please her husband (1 Cor 7:33-34).

The husband and wife both positively seek the other's best. Life decisions will always keep in mind what 'pleases' the other spouse, whether it be sex, relocation, purchases, etc. Marriage brought the male and female together so that they no longer live according to their own preferences but for the other.

Difficult marriages

Bad marriages wrestle with control issues. Each spouse is focused on their own "rights," and having their own demands or desires fulfilled. In great marriages, however, each has willingly given up his or her own preferences in order to pursue a greater good, that is, what is best for the other. This commitment at the same time builds up the marriage itself. Being a growing Christian fully complements the needs of a great marriage. For example, a Christian has died to serving himself and is committed to serving Christ. He serves Christ by serving others and in particular his or her partner.

A good example is the action between two magnets. Opposite poles attract. Similar poles repel. Line the poles up in the same direction, and they will stick to each other. But if you turn them north against north, then the magnets will repel each other. You can force them together, but they will still fight each other's presence. In the same way, intimacy takes advantage of the attraction. It works by the power of surrender. Intimacy helps you "stick" to one another. In order to judge your intimacy, ask yourself, "Do my decisions and attitudes bring blessings to my spouse?"

Last night our family came home late. The children had just finished climbing into bed. My wife said she was tired. She looked tired. But I saw more than this. I saw that she was so tired that she just wanted to forget about cleaning up the kitchen. She usually musters up the extra energy to clean up. I told her I would clean up the pans. We had rushed out of the house after supper. These pans were the most difficult pans to clean. Some were filled with fat (broiler pan) and others had burnt food caked on the edges. This was not my duty, but I knew I could help her in a significant way by voluntarily taking on the job. She went off to sleep. I took joy in cleaning pans for her and cleaning the kitchen counter. I respect her desire to come down to a clean kitchen in the morning. I helped her to accomplish that goal without further exhausting herself.

True intimacy has a lot to do with how much we share our heart with our spouse. This sharing is contingent upon the depth of the spouses' commitment to each other. Conversations and experiences must bring the couple together in such a way that they think and live as one. Let's further explore this in a fun way. Let's end this section by taking a seven-question intimacy quiz. See how intimate you are with your spouse. Answer 'Y' for yes and 'N' for no.

An Intimacy Quiz

Y N 1. You have spent more than 15 minutes at any one time in the last three days having a pleasant conversation with your spouse.

Y N 2. Can you name the two most important things on the mind of your husband or wife?

Y N 3. Do you feel fulfilled and at peace ten minutes after sexual intercourse?

Y N 4. Has the husband shared and discussed his future dreams in the last three months?

Y N 5. Do you like being alone with your spouse walking and talking?

Y N 6. Do you sense that there are no barriers between you?

Y N 7. In the last week have you consciously restrained your words in order to speak nicely to your spouse?

How did you do? If your marriage is intimate, your answers in a typical week should be yes. If your hearts are one, then your wills are one. You are soul mates. Much sharing takes place between you. Your desire to share your lives together is not supposed to stop after the honeymoon! Intimate couples strategically set aside time to be together. Growing their relationship is a priority.

B) Growing in Intimacy

Many couples wistfully remember those sweet, innocent times before marriage when they were so interested in each other. They would go out of their way just to see each other. How does a couple get back to that state? In one sense you can't because your motivation is not the same. In another sense, however, you can.

As the intimacy quiz revealed, you need to prioritize time to grow together. You actually need to carve out time in your schedule to be together. It is a simple act of obedience for the husband to cleave to or cherish his wife. He will spend time with her to 'know' her more. This time will need to be cut out of other segments of life such as entertainment and work. Parents may need to reduce some of the time used carting the children to their many activities.

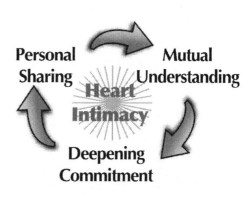

Your relationship will become a priority.

Some might base their decision to spend time talking with his or her spouse on whether they want to. If he or she does not feel like doing it, then he or she simply does not follow up on it. Instead, base your decision to communicate with your spouse on your general marriage commitment. The feelings will follow the right decisions, not vice-a-versa.

These three components to a growing marriage will develop this idea more: personal sharing, mutual understanding and deepening commitment.[55] It is a cycle that goes round and round, growing deeper with each round. Let's look at these three important aspects of growing an intimate marriage.

• Personal sharing

If a couple would just talk more to each other, they would grow in their intimacy. Clearly, a major challenge to intimacy in our modern world is busyness. As long as a man and a woman allow their times together to be leftovers from the busy world, they may as well assume that there will not be much growth.

---

[55] These thoughts have come from reflecting on spiritual and marital relationships along with observations from the scriptures.

Linda and I got hooked on spending an hour every evening talking and praying together before we were married. It has become the best of habits. This evening appointment has been the best thing for us.

In the beginning it was the only time I could see her. I would visit her at her parents' house. We spent our time together in Bible study, prayer and sharing. After we got married, it just continued on. Our marriage keeps getting better every year. Our marriage is so wonderful that it is hard to imagine that it could actually get even better, but each passing proves that it can.

Conversation between spouses must be honest, other-focused and true. Let us explain.

An honest conversation eliminates pretense. We do not need to pretend all is well when it is not. In fact, we are dishonest if we allow our spouse to think so. Our job is to help our spouse know who we really are. We might share our personal struggles with jealousy, pornography, or anger. When we take that honest step forward, the veil of secrecy falls away, and we can grow in intimacy. We cannot be close to a 'pretend' person. It is not his real person. Most conversations are shallow because they are not honest. It is fine to talk about buildings, races and school, but in the end, we need to share about our real hurts, hopes, desires and frustrations. This is where and when genuine growth begins to take place.

Conversation must be other-focused. Just as conversation can be superficial, it also can be selfish. If you always talk about yourself rather than inquiring into the life and concerns of your spouse, then you no longer need to wonder why your friendship with your spouse does not grow. No one likes people who like to talk only about themselves. This is true in a marriage too. The person who focuses on himself is content with only knowing himself. If there is something needed from the spouse, it is only to be a listening post. We are not speaking of how much a person speaks but whether he actually employs his words to  discover more about the other person. This is simple love. Intimacy by necessity demands an ongoing investigation into the life of one's spouse. We want to explore our spouse's life because we are interested in his or her person. Just the other night, I asked my wife to tell me something I did not know about her. She had to think long time but in the end came up with something.[56]

Our conversation must be true. Honesty and truth are admittedly very closely related. We want to separate them a bit to help us identify a problem many marriages have. Usually when a person thinks of honesty, he is only thinking whether or not his words are honest. Truth, however, reaches a deeper level. Truth goes deeper than words so one can know (*yadah*) what the other feels and thinks.

There are many things that a spouse might like or dislike, but not mention. Think about the things that you could do together. Out of politeness, you might not mention something you don't like. You just put up with it. You might think that your refraining from mentioning it is more loving, but because of the closeness of this relationship, you need a better approach, a more genuine approach. (If you are willing to

---

[56] One of our daughters is courting. She and her friend created a game that can be easily played by married couples. They called it 'Jeopardy' after the game show. One person asks a question about themselves and the other attempts to answer. Then the other person must answer the same question. They take turns initiating the question.

go but don't want to, you can mention it. "I know how much you like this. Why don't we go together!")

Personal sharing

For example, men and women are very different. We differ in how we experience and perceive life. My wife likes her back scratched. What good would it do if I scratched around the itchy place but never really scratched it. I do not want her quiet politeness, but a bit of guidance instead such as, "Could you move down to the left a little?" I love to hear, "Oh, yes!" Then I know that the itchy spot has been scratched.

Quiet politeness is not true enough. I understand that we do not want to offend but rather want to please the other. It is good to think about the other person; timing is important. But if something he or she does to give you pleasure does not really please you, speak up. If this was a momentary thing, then we could set this aside, but marriage is for life. Allow the relationship to grow in truth. "Speaking the truth in love" (Ephesians 4:15).

Conversing with our spouse is the most basic step that enables us to know how he or she thinks about or perceives different issues. We are beginning to know how our spouse is motivated. We gain insight into his or her struggles and temptations. As we gain more knowledge about them, we can better serve and care for them, and gain support from them.[57] Personal sharing leads us to mutual understanding.

---

[57] In our spiritual relationship with the Lord, it is important simply to talk and listen to the Lord through prayer and meditation on His Word.

• Mutual Understanding

Mutual understanding

Depth of personal conversation allows us to dive deeper into the lives and experiences of our spouse. Sometimes when my wife feels she is not able to tell me the whole story, she will write it down in a page or two and hand it to me. This is one way to solve the problem. In this way she can quietly focus on the issue, and I do not interrupt her thought process. She also has a chance before the Lord to clarify her own thoughts.

As a husband and wife begin to share more about their lives, they are able to better perceive who their spouse really is. The husband cannot love well if he does not know how his wife really thinks about a certain matter. The wife cannot be a good helpmate if she does not know well what God is doing in her husband's life. It is here that we learn as a couple that we are one and can make ourselves vulnerable to each other without destabilizing the relationship.

I believe it is here that the wife's "spots and wrinkles", as the apostle Paul says, are eliminated. Through the husband's unconditional love, his wife is able to open up more and more like a beautiful rose.

> *"Husbands, love your wives, just as Christ also loved the church and gave Himself up for her; that He might sanctify her, having cleansed her by the washing of water with the word, that He might present to Himself the church in all her glory, having no spot or wrinkle or any such thing; but that she should be holy and blameless" (Ephesians 5:25-27).*

Mutual understanding has one great side benefit that we are often oblivious to. It cripples the evil one's tactic of using misunderstandings and false assumptions to stir up mistrust. The better the husband and wife genuinely know (*yadah*) each other, the less they will misunderstand the other person's motives. When one's past is fully revealed to the other, then he or she knows they are fully accepted, just as they are by the Lord. The threat of blackmail is removed (i.e. What if he or she discovers ... will he or she still love me?). Nothing is hidden any more. This is much like relaxing one's muscles.

Relaxation cannot take place when the muscles are all tense. In order to reach relaxation, one has to mentally command the muscles to relax. (Try it. Tell yourself to relax your shoulder muscles. You will feel your shoulders slump a bit.) In a similar manner, a couple cannot fully take on the new form of oneness until they have dropped all of their reservations.

Some of these concerns and doubts have lingered in their minds for many years. The wife, for example, might be able to submit to her husband in all areas but one. However, she hesitates in that one area because she cannot quite trust him. The husband likewise might love his wife in all areas but holds back in one matter because he feels that she may misuse his love. More than likely there are even more areas, but until they progress past that block, they cannot rightly perceive all of their needs.

Holding back full trust shows that 'tense' parts of one's personal life still remain. These are fears and worries.[58] Fears cripple mutual understanding through misunderstanding and ignorance. Faith on the other hand freely encourages the couple to open up their lives to each other.

Intimate marriages are formed by the unconscious deepening of trust in each other. Intimacy is normal and good. As trust deepens, the Lord enables you to grow into the oneness that He declared on your wedding day. The word "know" is significant. Communication speaks

---

[58] Please remember that many fears and worries are learned from our parents, and we have wrongly anticipated these same situations with our spouse. As we get to share more our mutual understand allows us to grow. If we do not share, then the fears will lay beneath the surface and not be uncovered.

about revelation. Understanding addresses the issue of trust, accepting the knowledge into oneself and adjusting one's perspective.

As one better understands the other, they can begin to work, share and love together more closely. They like being 'one' and sharing their hearts and lives.

Shared knowledge enables the couple to increase their trust in one another and thereby grow in mutual understanding. Mutual understanding also protects you from many schemes of the devil. Satan uses misunderstanding to cause conflict between the two. With mutual understanding a couple is able to take deeper steps of commitment.

• Deepening Commitment

Just as a child cannot grow into an adult overnight, so a couple cannot mature in their intimacy through one or two special experiences like a wedding. It is a life-long process. A couple must engage in tens of thousands of special conversations and shared experiences for mutual trust to grow. Fears are overcome and replaced with an invigorating confidence in each other. As a result of this deepening mutual understanding, a firmer commitment evolves. This commitment is a bit different than most commitments. It is more subtle and unconscious but real.

Deepening commitment

This commitment shows itself in being one-hearted, willingness to sacrifice and a fond cherishing of each other.

One-hearted. A couple must increasingly come to the point where they have only one love. They are committed to each other and no other. This will show itself by putting aside fascinations and fantasies.

Even if one spouse has a disgusting habit, the other still resolves to be committed to loving his or her spouse. Jesus says that any sexual desire for another spouse is adultery. One-heartedness removes those uncommitted areas so that one spouse can fully cherish his or her mate.

Willing to sacrifice. Once committed, the spouse is further willing to sacrifice him or herself to care for the other. This is the spouse's life. Their faithfulness to bettering their spouse is more important than their own self. A couple in this way builds a great marriage, step by step. The husband's love will be broader and penetrate deeper. The wife's submission will be more genuine and propelled by a spirit of volunteerism.

More fond. With commitment, we gain a deeper sense of being accepted and cherished. The more we resolve to love our spouse, the more excitement and joy comes from the relationship. We are excited to see our spouse grow and be helped in some area. Our spouse's welfare becomes most important to us. So I pray for my spouse. I just sent an e-card to my wife who has not been feeling well.

This deeper commitment is in essence love. Love is the expression of unconditional, genuine concern for the other. Love is not merely a theory but is practical, kind and forgiving. Love is the underlying devotion toward each other that generates a host of kind words, generous actions and special favors.

These commitments are not often spoken of or even noticed by the individual spouse, but they occur. It allows the marriage to swing over into another cycle of growth. The husband and wife are more true and honest in their conversation. The whole cycle repeats itself.

Conclusion

An intimate marriage is characterized by the understanding that my spouse is vitally important to me. We are not just meeting each other's basic needs. We have come to believe, on the authority of God's Word, that our union is more blessed than our separateness. As we become convinced of our spouse's value to our lives, we are willing to bridge the big gender gaps so that we can really 'know' our spouses.

The more I believe my wife is important to my welfare, the more I will try to understand who she is and how she can help me in my life. The wife, in a similar way, will be able to further commit herself to her husband in a trusting manner. Confidence in God's design shapes our attitudes and actions.

Marital intimacy is sharing at the heart level. It takes time and purposeful genuine communication to reach there, but it is the path to walk down. Each spouse is convinced of the other's importance and so wonderfully treats his spouse. Each realizes that God has specially gifted their mate to work with him or her. It is only this confidence that compels them to change habits in order to take those steps toward deeper intimacy. Every step of commitment brings a deeper appreciation from the other spouse. This brings forth further changes in how they share their life.

Questions for Developing Intimacy

+ Have you carved out regular time in your schedule to devote to growing an intimate relationship with your spouse? Explain.

+ Would you say your conversations with your spouse are superficial or about matters of the heart?

+ Do you wonder whether or not you married the right person or have you wholeheartedly dedicated yourself to being a blessing to your spouse? If so, how have you shown this?

Troubled about Intimacy?

There are no doubt many questions that come to mind as we speak of making ourselves vulnerable to our spouses. One wife cannot trust her husband for anything let alone share her heart. Another wife has an adulterous husband. Is she to pretend he is faithful? Another couple is filled with bitterness. They are all asking whether intimacy is even possible. And like before, we will answer no, but there is an option that holds great hope.

You can choose to be inviting or to push him away. Words, attitudes and actions display the desire for a warm and beautiful marriage. A spouse cannot be forced to respond, but you can create an atmosphere that would cause your mate to want to be closer to you. On the other hand, you can chase your spouse away through a cold, sour, or condemning attitude.

A million housewives can (and do!) complain about their husbands' defects. You can join them and treat your husband as an enemy rather than as a friend. If he is treated like an enemy, he will act like the enemy. Much of the time we just do not recognize how much our own bad attitudes have poisoned our relationship.

What a difference it would make, if you would swallow your complaints, forgive him and start treating him as the Lord told you to with a gentle and quiet spirit. Only then will your husband realize that he likes to be home! Only when you are convinced that you both are on the same side, will you put away your critical remarks and thoughts and renew your commitment to oneness. It is only then that you can begin to undress your soul before your spouse and genuinely 'know' him or her.

And I know that there are just as many husbands who would wish they were married to someone else. And as long as you wish this, you wish evil. You will remain in the wild frustration of never being fulfilled. Instead of settling down and working hard to love this one woman for the rest of your life, you are looking at all the reasons she does not deserve your love. You can stay like that or you can begin to increase the level of trust. Then she can slowly (it will seem like forever) be disarmed from her mistrust. She senses that she is not desired so she does not make herself desirable. Desire her, not only for her body but also for who she is, and she will begin to respond.

Many marriages, as indicated above, are crippled and continue on at superficial levels. They are happy just sharing a house in peace. God wants so much more. God wants us to go deeper and deeper in the levels of intimacy. There we have more freedom to reveal our deepest selves to our spouse.

C) Sexual intimacy

Couples are willing to use sex to satisfy their immediate physical needs. The husband has strong physical urges; the wife has a deep need to feel wanted. The physical relationship gives them a little of what they want but more often than not, the sex act only reminds them of what they really do not have.

"How beautiful you are!"
"My darling."
"How beautiful you are!"
"Your eyes are like doves."
Song of Solomon 1:15

If the physical relationship is not built on a good social relationship and marriage commitment, then old feelings of bitterness and guilt will return after sex. Even sex can bring its own guilt because it is used in a selfish way to fulfill one's own needs.

What should the sexual relationship be like? Physical intimacy must be built on the foundation of a good marriage relationship where the couple reveals their soul to one another. We are not just speaking of consent or willingness, but a heart united in the 'knowing' of each other. Sex then is not a goal to reach. It is a deeper and more beautiful expression of the union they already have. The extremely pleasant feelings and fulfilled urges blend together in a masterpiece of oneness.

Many couples never get beyond serving their own needs. Sex for them is about getting what they need rather than giving to the other. There is a world of difference between being used and being loved. There is a great difference between a marriage where the husband is fascinated with and completely taken with his wife and one in which the husband fantasizes about other women. Does the husband really love his wife? Is he really focused on her?

Some of the greatest tests will come in bed with her. Let's look at a few examples. He has his plans for the evening, but she is not feeling well, is tired or perhaps her period (time of the month) just started. Will he be patient or irritated? Will he state through his words and actions that her welfare is more important than satisfying his desires. Or in another situation, what if she simply turns her back on him because she is resentful over something he said to her in the morning? How will the husband respond? Will his focus be more on fulfilling his own sexual longings or on deepening his relationship with her? Each time he denies himself for her, she deepens her trust for him. She acknowledges that he loves her just for who she is and not for what she can give. (What if she gets old and she can't give any more?)

The wife has her own tests too. The command to be submissive is not easy when your husband is insensitive! If she remains resentful, she will convey her unwillingness to be intimate with him. Even if she makes herself willing, she is not much of a companion.

The bed often becomes a battlefield. Each side is struggling. The wife needs to find forgiveness for her bitterness and welcome her husband rather than shun him even in his selfish moments. Non-Christian husbands are not thinking of Christ when they go to the bedroom. She needs to be gentle and of a quiet demeanor even in bed. If there he finds a most gracious and kind woman, his heart will slowly be changed (see 1 Peter 3:1).

Only by being faithful to our calling, will we be able to take the marriage forward. Bed habits are not excluded. Even if our spouses are stubborn, foolish or lazy, we need to love that one to whom we have committed ourselves. Some might say it is impossible. It would be more correct to say it is impossible without Christ, but it is possible to love like Christ through His Holy Spirit. We can forgive others and decidedly give to them the good they do not deserve.

It is unfortunate that not everyone has a truly intimate relationship based on a deep commitment to each other. The only way to start going that way is for you who are responsive to God to begin being fully faithful to your spouse. Make no excuses. Pray and fast if needed. Be determined that, even if your spouse never rightly responds, you will be his or her faithful partner. I believe the spouse in most situations will respond. That is why you got married. A person's faithfulness brings hope back into the marriage for it acts as a channel of God's mighty love.

Some people believe that the sexual act is for self-fulfillment. That is totally untrue. The sexual act is designed to fulfill your mate. We are to focus on the other's needs rather than on our own. What about you? God has designed to take care of our needs as we devotedly serve others. This is a way we must trust in the Lord.

Genuine love is greatly needed in bed. Patience, kindness, and forgiveness will create wonderful times together. Only with God's love, can the husband be willing to go without sex if necessary. Only God's graciousness will allow the wife to open her body to her husband even if he has recently treated her unkindly.

The husband is not to rush for his pleasure and ignore her needs. Women respond more slowly. So husbands need to take things slower so they can focus on their wife's needs. The wife must also be aggressive in pleasing her husband. They need honest and true conversation combined with cushions of love to reach the maximum feelings of delight.

These things might be easy to suggest or say, but I do realize that at many times we will need to cry out to God for help. Only He only can help. That is fine. Our Lord loves to hear our prayers. He wants to be seen as 'our refuge.' We will need help for ourselves to rightly respond, especially when we do not feel like it. We will need His help to change our spouse's heart and choices. We will need help to wait for Him to answer!

Questions on Developing Sexual Intimacy

1. Would you say that you focus on fulfilling your spouse's needs during sex or your own?

2. How do you respond as a husband to your wife when she puts you off for reasons of sickness, inconvenience, tiredness or from being upset?

3. How should you respond to your husband if you are not sexually interested?

4. Why should a Christian spouse still dedicate him or herself to her mate?

D) The Purpose of Intimacy

A marriage can run into a rut if it does not grow in intimacy and oneness. Intimacy, however, is not a final goal. It is the means to accomplishing God's purpose for your life.

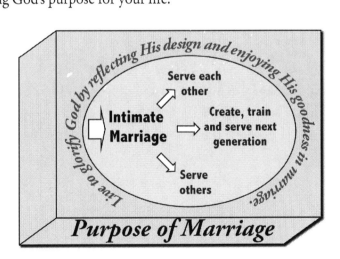

Marriage has a purpose beyond itself. An individual exists for more than eating and living. He has a purpose in life. The purpose of a factory is more than just providing a place for people to come and work. They are manufacturing items. God has designed marriage in a similar way. The purpose of marriage always goes beyond serving its own self.[59] Let us discuss three ways to extend our intimacy by serving others.

1) Serve your spouse

Marriage, as has already been mentioned, is an endless opportunity for the husband and wife to serve God as they serve each other. Since the relationship is so closely bound, they are tested and proven in ways that do not normally occur outside of marriage.

The husband must realize his golden opportunity to serve his wife. He must specialize in pleasing her by devotedly living for her. Don't worry; she won't object! Not only does he do things for her, but he also treasures her in his heart. He is quite willing to focus his undivided heart fully on her. He is content. This becomes his great privilege, joy and reward on earth.

"So husbands ought also to love their own wives as their own bodies. He who loves his own wife loves himself; for no one ever hated his own flesh, but nourishes and cherishes it, just as Christ also does the church, because we are members of His body" (Ephesians 5:28-30).

The wife also must realize that her golden opportunity to show her love to God will be in catching the vision of being a helpmate. She was designed for that key position. The many individual situations that arise go far beyond her feelings. They go right to the issue of obedience. From her faithful service, a beautiful glow from God will emanate from her life.

---

[59] God had perfect intimacy in the triune Godhead and yet extended Himself out into the world.

"For indeed man was not created for the woman's sake, but woman for the man's sake" (1 Corinthians 11:9).

"An excellent wife is the crown of her husband, But she who shames him is as rottenness in his bones" (Proverbs 12:4).

God does not want us to stop here in our service to ourselves. He demands that it go beyond this.

2) Serve your children

The most obvious fruit of the marriage relationship is children. Each child is a perfect fruit of the parents' oneness. God wants His people to have lots of children. He commands us, as married couples, to have the children He will give to us. The blessed home has many children. Even Joseph and Mary had at least five other children after having Jesus.

Intimate marriages naturally bear children.[60] We should warmly welcome God's hand in creating children. He alone opens and closes the womb. This life-giving intimacy includes not only the husband and wife but also God. We are open to what God wants. We live not for ourselves but for what He wants to do through our lives. Since this is a very un-predictable process, if we do not fully love and trust God, we tend to be fearful and anxious instead of confident and joyful.

Birth control has at least five obvious problems.

- 1) Man wants the privileges of marriage (sex) without its responsibili-ties (children).
- 2) Man thinks that a marriage without children is better than one

---

[60] There are special exceptions like Sara, Hannah and others who for special reasons could not have the children they desired. These couples must understand that God has some special plans for their lives.

with children. Fewer are better.

3) Man disobeys God by not bringing forth many children into the world.

4) Man often kills children in order to avoid having them.

5) Man thinks his plans for family planning are better than God's.

Many couples want more money and time to themselves. They decide not to have children. Marriage for them has become a selfish institution. It would be better not to marry.

Parents spend much of their lives caring for their children. This requires many years of investment. They must constantly and sacrificially give of their time, energy, body, money, and possessions in order to raise them for God. In a true sense, what they have as parents becomes their children's. We love this song of praise given to a faithful wife and mother.

> "She opens her mouth in wisdom, And the teaching of kindness is on her tongue. She looks well to the ways of her household, And does not eat the bread of idleness. Her children rise up and bless her; Her husband also, and he praises her, saying: "Many daughters have done nobly, But you excel them all." Charm is deceitful and beauty is vain, But a woman who fears the LORD, she shall be praised" (Proverbs 31:26-30).

Birth control is another one of the many ways that we hold on to our own selfish way of life and do not totally entrust our lives into God's hands. Preventing conception means that we lock God out of this area of our life. When we say "no" to God in this area, we are in essence limiting our ability to be intimate with our spouse. My wife and I have been on both sides of this fence, so to speak. We have a gap of seven years between our second and third children. This is partly due to using birth control methods. We can testify that once we were able, by God's grace, to throw out our birth control paraphernalia that God brought our marriage to a deeper and more intimate level. We learned to trust God together. We had more freedom to fully open our lives before Him.

3) Serve your world

Marriage is for channeling God's love to the world. God-designed marriage is the place that the world sees true love in action.. Marriage is all about serving, not being served. The joys of marriage will only reach the husband and wife that are committed to serving those around them. As a family they will extend God's goodness and love into the world by service to others.

This can take many forms, but it starts by loving your neighbors and the people you meet. Sometimes a husband and wife are too busy making money or taking their children to their activities to have their house be a home. Families need to slow way down to enable them to make room for service. Are there not many people that need a home away from home? Maybe God would want to use your family to minister to these people.

We also suggest praying together about how God wants to use you in this world. We will often miss God's best simply because we have not asked Him. Think about each of your gifts and burdens (concerns). How does God want to use these to bring a greater blessing to the world? But maybe you have unidentified gifts that He is still unwrapping. Keep praying and seeking Him. He often opens doors that we never even knew were there!

The Focus on Him

As we open our lives to the Lord, we begin to glorify Him. Each issue that we deal with ultimately becomes one in which we battle over glorifying God or not. Obedience is an issue of trust. When we trust or believe Him, we deepen our lives with Him and our spouse. Marriage is a place that God wants to make His glory known. He wants us to have beautiful marriages so that others can see the awe of oneness and catch a glimpse of God's person and the way He wants to be intimate with God's people. Marriage is a wonderful institution.

Questions about Serving Others

1. Have you ever thought about yourselves as a couple (or family) in light of serving others?

2. Have you sought the children God would give to you to accomplish His greater purposes?

3. Have you given in to birth control (family planning)? Why? How might you change it?

4. For the next week give praise to God for three ways He has been glorified through the way you handled things in your marriage.

A Question about Intimacy

A natural question arises when talking about service. Should we have any time left for ourselves as a couple? With caring for young children, and dad busy at church and work, there are times when it seems impossible for a couple to get together. Emergencies do arise and require separation, but they are times of emergency not the norm. A wife working far away in another city is not an emergency. The wife is made for the husband. She should be at his side. Careers for women have fouled up God's plans for marital intimacy.

It is important and vital to make some time together on a regular and frequent basis. We do our best to go out once a week without the children. Linda likes me to plan these times, or at least state that it is important to me by saying when we will go out that week. I now understand why (it has taken many years to finally understand this). She doesn't just want to be with me, she also wants to know that I desire to be with her. My planning initiative adds the needed special touch.

Lately, she has been concerned about going out at noon on Fridays. She knows I teach Friday nights and might be distracted or busy preparing materials. I arrange things in such a way that I am not distracted. Otherwise, our time together would not serve to build the relationship.

Do we need to spend a lot of money? No. In fact money often gets in the way of relationship. At times we have had picnics together followed by a walk. These have been some of the sweetest times (if no active allergies interfere).

Summary

Any marriage that looks at itself in the mirror too long will begin to age and decay. We are here to serve others: our spouse, our children and others. By serving others, we are glorifying God.

I personally might be off teaching somewhere while she stays home to care for the children. In fact we are serving together. We must not think one type of service is less important than the other. The reward we will receive is based on heart attitude and on acts of service in the context in which God has placed us. We are serving together. We use our intimacy in marriage to be a lighthouse of truth, a fire of glowing love and a place to build trust.

We will need to live by faith to reach that great marriage. We need to rigorously live by God's standards rather than our feelings. But step by step, as our hearts unfold, the beauty of marriage blossoms into a deep, enriching and intimate marriage.

Chapter #8 Study Questions

1. Is the term 'intimacy' biblical? Where does it come from?

2. What word does the Old Testament use to describe sexual relationships? What else does it mean?

3. How does intimacy show itself in a Christian's relationship with Christ?

4. How did you do on the intimacy quiz? What one area do you need to work on most?

5. What surprised you most about the four principles from 1 Corinthians 7:33:34 regarding married couples?

6. What are the three parts of growing intimacy for a married couple?

7. What is one key for a fulfilling sexual relationship?

8. What is the purpose of intimacy?

9. Share three areas that this purpose can be expressed.

10. How can a couple develop their communication skills to better know his or her spouse?

11. Birth control holds back marital intimacy. What are three reasons family planning is contrary to God's purpose?

Building a
Great Marriage

#9 Developing Trust & Intimacy

No book has affected my life more than the Song of Solomon. For any book to so impact a person's life there must have been significant changes. This has certainly been true in my case. Nobody, however, could observe the deep foundational changes that were slowly taking place deep within me.

God's Word again has proven how it provides an unending mine of riches enabling us to dig for whatever our soul needs. The Song of Songs contains nuggets of gold that unlock the mystery of love, intimacy and trust. These nuggets are the keys to a growing marriage.

In other books of the Bible, we have commands and illustrations that instruct us on how to have a good marriage. If we would obey them, we would do well. But there are other things that keep us from having confidence in His commands. We do not really believe they work. We should not have this perspective, but many do. Our lack of confidence is one major reason we do not carry them out and because of disobedience, our marriages suffer.

There is an increasing number of marriage problems surfacing all about us. It seems that each week I am made aware of another layer of significant marital difficulties that people are facing. Your experience is probably similar.

My marriage would have suffered the same devastation had it not been for the power of God's Word that was revealed during times of meditation on the Song of Solomon. I was not planning to study this book but at the last minute in January 1975, thanks to the prompting of the Spirit of God, I did. My life has been greatly changed.

I must admit that not all the changes and main impact came immediately, but what will be shared below are the truths that set a foundation by which all the changes could be made. Maybe you wonder what it was that made such a difference in my life.

I suppose most basically it had to do with a change in how I perceived myself. Everyone wants acceptance, and I was no different. Relationships enable a person to see himself from a different perspective. Loving relationships enable a person to look through the other person's eyes at his own life and gain a more accurate picture.

Stained Relationships

I never learned about warmth and acceptance growing up. Divorce, bitterness and criticism left my family and me emotionally crippled. I could not easily relate to others. I personally faced a number of problems including stammering and other forms of insecurity. The problems children face from growing up in dysfunctional families are becoming more manifest as the number of marriages suffering such traumas increase. In study after study, these developmental problems are being identified.

The Song of Solomon came into my life like a breath of fresh air. Helping to unlock the ideas in that book was my girlfriend, now my wife. I was desperate for her smile even though most of our close friendship was separated by a thousand miles. I can see why I thrived under the light of her warm smile. Her acceptance and desire for my companionship meant so much to me. It was the same truth that God began to vividly teach me in the scriptures – God's love.

The question was how would God instill this knowledge of love in me. God's love is ever present, but inward voices persuaded me that I was unwanted and inadequate. Satan interfered with my rightly comprehending the love streaming from God and others. Of course, when one feels unloved, he is afraid to expose his true self to others for fear of rejection.

What usually happens, and would have happened to me, is that my responses would have been so self-absorbed by my perception of myself that I would have destroyed any relationship that I became involved in. And this is what happens to many children who are brought up in bad marriages. They end up having worse relationships with their spouses than their parents.

Only God's grace and wisdom has kept me from being another statistic. Let me go on and share how our most gracious Lord did this. I may be oversimplifying the process, but the keys that unlocked certain doors of understanding in my life ushered me into places I would never otherwise have been able to reach. You can use these keys too. Let's first pray.

> *"Dear Lord, would you please break through our stubborn and blind hearts. We don't deserve your love. We can't even understand it. Much like the sun, it is so bright that we have put on sunglasses to keep its light out. We have learned to live in the shadows of darkness rather than the glories of your love. Bring us close, dear Lord, bring us closer to you so that we in turn can have great marriages. In Christ's Glorious Name we pray, Amen.*

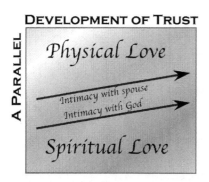

The Song of Solomon played a key role in changing my life. There are certain verses that God used to show me that I was loved and accepted. When a child grows up with criticism and bitterness, he does not really know what love is. This child has an inner life of bitter secrets and angry solitude. Things might appear to be fine on the outside, but there are problems within. These problems become more apparent in relationships with others and especially in marriage.

The Song of Solomon has two sets of three verses that describe love and a growing trust. The first triad is taken from the first section (1:1-3:5) of the book. It discusses the courtship or budding romance of the couple. The second triad is spread over the whole of the Book of Solomon. One of these verses is in both triads.

Part of the powerful way God injected me with these truths was through the fact that our relationship with Him parallels the relationship of a man and woman who meet, enter marriage and live together as one. At this point in my life I loved God with an inferior love. I also held deep hopes of marrying once out of college. Each verse of the triad unlocks certain key perspectives that are needed in a growing an intimate relationship. This is true both with the Lord as well as with our mate. Let's take a look at them.

Triad #1: The Path of Trust

We will find this first triad of verses in 1:5, 2:1 and 2:16. Each statement is a reflection of the bride-to-be. She is reflecting on herself in light of her man's love for her (though it seems that in 1:5 and 2:16 he was not actually there in her presence). Men might feel a little awkward learning from the bride. They think, "I'm no bride" and simply turn off. But hold on.

Remember that this book is written from both a spiritual and physical perspective. In this case, when the bride is speaking, think of yourself as the bride of Christ. The man, loving the woman, represents Christ showing His love for the church. The bride-to-be represents all Christians. As Ephesians 5 says, the church is the bride of Christ. This will help us cross some gender gaps that would otherwise keep these truths from seizing our hearts.

Accepted > Valued > Belonging

1) Accepted (Song of Solomon 1:5)

I am black but lovely, O daughters of Jerusalem, Like the tents of Kedar, Like the curtains of Solomon. Do not stare at me because I am swarthy, For the sun has burned me. My mother's sons were angry with me; They made me caretaker of the vineyards, But I have not taken care of my own vineyard (Song of Solomon 1:5-6).

The key phrase is, "I am black but lovely." Through these words and the following explanation we observe her initial perception of herself. In the following verses we trace her developing perception of herself.

I carefully use the word 'perception' because what we believe about ourselves is not always true. For example, we are sinners but many peo-

---

Perception

What I perceive about myself is often not true. It is the truth of God that sets us free.
His perception of us is what is right and real. We need to acquire these truths.

Perception of Self		God's Perception of Us	
Wrong	We believe that we are not that bad.	**Right**	We are totally unacceptable before God because of our sin.
Wrong	We feel clumsy, rejected and lonely.	**Right**	As valuable creatures we are designed with a purpose.

---

ple deny it. On the other hand, we might feel clumsy and lonely and yet are valuable creatures designed with a purpose. What I perceive about myself is often not true. It is the truth of God that sets us free. His perception of us is what is right and real. It is these truths that we need to acquire to gain a right perspective of Him as well as ourselves. The question is "How?"

Many Christians have heard about the love of God but seem untouched by it. They think they deserve God's love. They get angry at events in their lives that seem to cast doubt on God's love for them. These people are very different from this maiden. They would not say 'I am black but lovely,' but 'I am fair and lovely.' I had no problem with starting here!

God had already revealed my horrible selfishness and sins when He saved me. Later, He showed me in His Word how accurate His perspective of my sinful life was. I truly was filled with pride, selfishness and a long list of attitudes and behaviors that did not glorify God.

There are two approaches to self-understanding. They make a key difference in a person's life. Jesus starts off with the same approach in His famous *Sermon on the Mount*, "Blessed are the poor in spirit." (Matthew 5:3)

Whether or not we accept the facts about our sinful lives greatly shapes how we approach life. The bride openly admitted how 'tarnished' she looked. Her skin was burnt due to working hard in the vineyards.[61] She did not have the means to protect her skin by being brought up in the palace, but being of lower class she worked hard outside. And even more specifically, she was the lowest in the family because she did the hard work herself. In a spiritual sense the 'dark' represents her unworthiness to be loved by Christ due to her sin.

> *Do not stare at me because I am swarthy, for the sun has burned me. My mother's sons were angry with me; they made me caretaker of the vineyards.*

In order to flush out the real meaning of these two views of acceptance, let us look at the differences side by side.

Godly view	Secular view
"I am dark but lovely."	*"I am fair and lovely."*
Humility: Recognizes one's own faults.	**Superficial**: Focus is on self; less intimate because more independent.
Undeserving: Appreciative of attention because it is not thought to be deserved. Source of attention is outside self.	**Deserving**: Attention and adoration is to be expected because the source is inside oneself.
Retainable: Independent of one's beauty, age or gifts; it is because she is chosen.	**Vulnerable:** Is dependent on temporal, fading things.
Secure: Does not seek affirmation but delights in and is thankful for any received affection.	**Insecurity**: Seeks affirmation; anxious if not received because the relationship depends on the temporal.

All relationships start off superficial. The guy and gal are just getting to know each other in the beginning. As the couple gets better ac-

---

[61] Please do not draw the erroneous conclusion that she was unlovely because she was black from Africa. The context clearly teaches that her dark skin is from working in the field.

quainted, however, the relationship ought to become more deep and personal. They should reveal intimate things of their hearts. When a person starts a relationship with the belief that a person's attention to her is dependent upon something she is or has, then that relationship remains very superficial.

As a result of this, the person cannot focus on serving the other but must constantly figure out ways to get attention and affirmation. Because the relationship is not perceived to be founded on unconditional acceptance, it seems shaky. As long as the relationship is perceived as unstable, then all one's energy goes to protecting it. Petty jealousies, suspicious attitudes, demand for time and gifts are a few manifestations of this.

Insecure relationships therefore cause perpetual crises, so to speak, characterized by fears, worries and superficial relationships. These inner strivings wear the body and the relationship down. They do not foster the vulnerability needed for the development of mutual trust. The friendship is awkward and can never penetrate the superficial. The basic underlying reason for this guarded approach is to secure the relationship as much as possible.

Put a check mark next to key elements for a good marriage that are true for you.

- [ ] • Humility: Accepts one's fault and apologizes.
- [ ] • Appreciation: Receives love as undeserved.
- [ ] • Accepted: At peace, unthreatened, calm and joyful.
- [ ] • Responsive: Responds to love by loving gestures.
- [ ] • Trusting: Believes his/her spouse really care.
- [ ] • Secure: Delights in partner's love and affection.

The person dares not fully reveal his or her own self for fear of rejection. Such women will base their acceptance on beauty and their fear on age and wrinkles. Trust therefore never grows. There is no intimate sharing from which great marriages can be formed.

When a person starts off right, however, a whole different set of principles is set in operation. Security in the relationship results in the development of a normal trusting relationship. The person can grow as the relationship grows.

Our Christian lives need a firm foundation too. Those who are not quite clear about their sin, are never very sure of their salvation. Early discipleship training should always include instruction about our sin and the gracious and effective work of Christ Jesus on our behalf.

She does not only say, "I am black." She says, "I am black but lovely." We are not to be preoccupied with our weaknesses. We are racked with problems. We are sinners, but something great has come into our lives despite our lowly origins. In the following verses we see all the maidens dancing for joy because she has been chosen. The king has set his heart on her.

This is why the commitment that is formalized in marriage is so important. The bridegroom has specially chosen her for life. He will bestow his full heart of affection upon her. She is set apart despite her inferior background. Her delight comes from her acceptance despite her obvious flaws.

The same is true for the spiritual as well as the earthly. The parallel relationships bring much clarity. Where we are weak in understanding one, we can learn from the other. For example, my family was broken, but I could learn of God's great love for me here from His Word.

We are not chosen because of any good in ourselves. Solomon had many to choose from, but he chose to put his favor on her (1:4b). He chose to delight in her. In a similar way, God in Christ has chosen us for Himself. He did not choose everyone. We are sinful and yet He chose us. Our salvation is not dependent upon what we do because our sin has marred everything. He has chosen the ungodly and wicked to become His special possession. Many Christians fight the teaching of election because they do not understand their 'blackness.'

The joy in our Christian lives starts when we can celebrate Christ's choice of us because He desired us to be with Him for eternity.

> *Blessed be the God and Father of our Lord Jesus Christ, who has blessed us with every spiritual blessing in the heavenly places in Christ, just as He chose us in Him before the foundation of the world, that we should be holy and blameless before Him. In love He predestined us to adoption as sons through Jesus Christ to Himself, according to the kind intention of His will, to the praise of the glory of His grace, which He freely bestowed on us in the Beloved (Ephesians 1:3-6).*

We might never understand why He would choose us, but let us move on and begin reveling in the thought! This is His acceptance of us in Christ. This also reveals why there is a command for husbands to consistently and devotedly love their wives. This is the reason the wife feels so good when her husband affirms his commitment to her through kind words and deeds. Those manifestations of his love remind her of something deeper, his special and life-long choice of her.

Everyone seeks for acceptance but those who do not feel accepted growing up (whether rightly perceived or not) desperately long for this acceptance. It is this deep desire for acceptance that has propelled these unprepared individuals into relationships and marriage. Without finding this acceptance, though, they find themselves scarred and yet driven to find another relationship that promises acceptance. I was one of them. Fortunately, the Lord taught me early on that the acceptance I really sought was in Christ and not in some human relationship which will never fully satisfy.

2) Valued (Song of Solomon 2:1)

Bride-to-be: I am the rose of Sharon, The lily of the valleys. (Song of Solomon 2:1)

Bridegroom-to-be: Like a lily among the thorns, So is my darling among the maidens. (2:2)

In between these three revelations of her self-awareness, there are lots of special words and activities going on between the couple. During this courtship phase the couple is 'in love.' As they exchange words, they grow in their intimacy. If married couples could just continue this kind treatment, so many problems would be solved! So what is it that we discover from the bride's response here in 2:1?

We no longer see her reminiscing about her blackness even though her skin no doubt is still darkened. The fears and terrors of rejection are past. She no longer thinks about those things. We can see what she is thinking from her words.[62] She now says of herself, "I am the rose of Sharon, the lily of the valleys."

Her understanding of herself has developed and now she begins to see herself as he sees her. She declares herself to be one of the beautiful flowers they have seen on the pathway, full of blended color and aroma. Warm with a soft touch. When a person finds acceptance, they can move on and begin to open their life for further growth. We start seeing ourselves as special and valuable.

---

[62] If we could only take an objective view of ourselves from the words we write, say and think, we would gain a great amount of insight about our inner struggles.

This is what he sees: her precious value. We can see this through the next verse. She stops at describing herself as a beautiful and desirable flower. He importantly does not stop there. He brings to her mind that she is "a lily among thorns." He affirms his delight in her. He states she is a lovely lily. But he goes beyond this and states that she is as a lily among thorns. He delights in his choice of her.

He not only states his commitment toward her but also expresses his affection for her. This unceasing affection continues right to the end of the book. It is not as if this man is blinded. No. There are many maidens around. Now it is one thing to hear how the maidens delight in his choice of her (1:4), but it is so much more wonderful to hear the man affirm that his sole delight is in her.

How do you determine value? How do you determine which car is the best? Do you not look around? Do you not compare and see how one model stacks up against the next? In the end he will stay satisfied because he has done the shopping. This man affirms that he has looked around. The other women are like unattractive 'thorns' compared to her, the 'lily.'

As he reveals his firm choice and delights in her, she further opens her heart to be showered and touched by the warm love being provided. He cherishes her; she responds. Her perception of herself is slowly being shaped from his affection for her. His choice of her lifts up her value. Those who love or are loved understand this. It is not false but true. Something special is happening. I believe this reflects back to a picture of the great and awesome love of God toward us. We have a difficult time grasping His love and need such pictures and experiences to awaken us to His great desire for us. His commitment and affection toward her properly shape the way she thinks of herself.

Practically speaking
Husbands need to affirm the special qualities of their wives. They love hearing how they are special in different areas. Proverbs 31 listed the

special deeds that made that woman outstanding. Whether it be a meal, a kind word or a smile, let her know how she specifically has been a blessing to you. When husbands express their delight in their wives, wives are able to respond with more trust. A husband's kind and appreciative words are like the sun which cause his wife's heart to more and more unfold like a flower.

I have found that my fondness of my wife grows as I focus on my commitment toward her. My value for her is not built on what she does but on my acceptance. If I switch them around by placing my acceptance on her value, then she gets insecure and the marriage begins to freeze up. Perhaps we can say that we should love for love's sake. Only when the sun shines does the flower unfold, and we see the precious value within.

Spiritually speaking

The Lord truly treasures us. He has not made a mistake. He has chosen us for eternity. This was not because of any good in us. We should not, however, conclude that He does not value us. Quite the opposite (and this is where some wrongly end up when they only think of their sin). His love awakens our responses to Him and because of His commitment to us, we become valuable to Him. He delighted to make us His own precisely because He did value our companionship. The key point here is that we stay His. We stay loyal to Him. We refuse to be caught by the lure of the world. We have one more step to go in this first triad.

3) Belonging (Song of Solomon 2:16)

My beloved is mine, and I am his (Song of Solomon 2:16a).

The woman is chosen. He affirms his choice of her alone. These things open the way for her to see how her identity is wrapped up in him. If we read the verses in between step #2 and #3, we can see why she might think this way!

My beloved responded and said to me, 'Arise, my darling, my beautiful one, and come along. For behold, the winter is past, the rain is over and gone. The flowers have already appeared in the land; the time has arrived for pruning the vines, and the voice of the turtledove has been heard in our land (Song of Solomon 2:10-12).

Intimacy is not a one-sided affair. In fact, we will see that this verse also serves as the first step of the second cycle. Steps of true intimacy between a man and a woman can only come after marriage. But in this cycle of courtship, the young lady begins to ready herself for marriage, which we will soon address in the next chapter. She is not talking about beauty any more. Her reference point becomes identification with him: possession and ownership.[63]

Value is one thing but ownership is the language of commitment. After the wedding, the sealing of the commitment, there is no turning back. The trust she has developed earlier has now enveloped her life. His acceptance of her has brought her to the point of oneness.

We do not see her saying these things directly to him. She is just catching some of her pre-wedding thoughts and putting them in a bottle for keeps.

Practically speaking

Some people wonder why marriage eliminates romance. It shouldn't. The purpose of romance is to bring one to a heightened life commitment. Marriage enables us to step into intimacy in a special lifelong guarded relationship where acceptance no longer needs to be questioned. (May we never threaten or contemplate divorce!)

Courtship enables us to catch a glimpse of a relationship that we would love to have. The wedding ushers us into marriage where we can and must daily bestow our affection and care for our mate and indeed receive our mate's care. If we find that we no longer value and treasure

---

[63] This is what Paul alludes to so strongly in 1 Corinthians 7:1-3.

our spouse, we need to go back and ask, "When did it stop?" "Why?" Perhaps we allowed an argument to make us somewhat forgetful (because of resentment) or to compromise on our promised love for our spouse.

Spiritually speaking

The Lord looks for our own commitment to Him. He 'bought us with a price.' There is no doubt about His commitment toward us. Jesus speaks about us being 'in Him' not once but over and over again. Nineteen times the phrases 'in Him' or 'in Christ' are used in Ephesians alone. The strength of our faith will depend on how much we actually perceive ourselves to be identified with Him (i.e. Christ).

> *In Him, you also, after listening to the message of truth, the gospel of your salvation--having also believed, you were sealed in Him with the Holy Spirit of promise (Ephesians 1:13).*

This first triad of verses focuses on the development of love and trust. The development of their relationship surged forward. True, it is only romantic and not tested by the trials of marriage (How do I respond when he or she does not love me as I think he or she should?). On the other hand, this pre-wedding development has enabled the couple to come to the point where they are desirous for each other and willing to be with each other for life.

This time of pre-marriage romance is designed to enhance the elements that build trusting relationships in a good marriage. The couple has moved a long way toward trusting each other in order to commit themselves to each other for life. The elements of trust include:

- ❖ An acceptance of each other the way they are
- ❖ A perpetual stream of kind words
- ❖ Exchanges of affectionate words
- ❖ A man's selective choice of the woman

❖ A treasuring of her above all others

❖ A surrender of self to become 'one' with the other

In marriage we die to our own concerns so that we can be faithful to the other. All other concerns must fall aside compared to this one. If this is the commitment made before the wedding, then we should have no doubts about how this trust will grow and develop. The seeds of trust that are planted early on must continue through spring showers, summer storms and bleak winters. If you can so treat and serve your spouse in such a manner before your marriage, you can afterwards too.

This beginning, though wonderful and beautiful, still cannot compare to the intimacy to come. Marriage is the starting point of a journey on the path of oneness where intimacy grows and flourishes. This is what we will observe in the second triad of verses.

Triad #2: The Path toward Intimacy

Let's look briefly at the second triad to help us see the growth of intimacy. Do remember that intimacy can grow only as much as trust has developed. Under the man's constant love, we find that the bride grows in her life through reflecting on herself in light of his love for her. It would seem that the maturing of reflective thought reaches its apex in 2:16 but clearly this is not so.

Song of Solomon's Two Triads

Triad #1: The Path of Trust (SS 1:5; 2:1; 2:16)	Triad #1 develops trust so that one spouse can unfold his or her heart to the other.
Triad #2: The Path toward Intimacy (SS 2:16; 6:3; 7:10)	Triad #2 clarifies the two transformations that enable a couple to reach that deep intimacy.

The progress becomes much more refined. Only the shared years and experiences that marriage provides can take the relationship further. Let's note the three similar verses. We will need to do some detective work.

"My beloved is mine, and I am his" (Song of Solomon 2:16).

"I am my beloved's and my beloved is mine" (Song of Solomon 6:3).

"I am my beloved's and his desire is for me" (Song of Solomon 7:10).

In order to see intimacy grow to what it should be, we start with a sincere commitment to each other. The bridegroom commits himself to love her unconditionally. The bride responds by entrusting herself to him. She takes on his name. She goes and lives with him. After the first step, that we will discuss briefly, we will note the two other transformations that take place in the spouse's mind and heart.

The Commitment (Song of Solomon 2:16)

"My beloved is mine, and I am his" (Song of Solomon 2:16).

In this case, the bride-to-be has found delight in having such a husband. She is focused on what she has found. She acknowledges that she belongs to him, but it is second in her mind. (Notice what she says first and second in these lines.) She thinks less of her ability, privilege or responsibility to serve him than his ability to keep, protect and provide for her. We are not saying that this is wrong. It only leaves much room for further growth and maturity. The first opening of a flower is still far from being in full blossom.

We have already shared the needed steps of growth that lead to the commitment to each other through marriage vows. Some couples get to this point, but they start off with the wrong assumptions: intimacy is based on attraction rather than commitment, beauty rather than choice. They seem to have a good relationship, but it becomes paralyzed by personal grudges, acts of selfishness and pride. Many times they do not want to recognize and deal with these insecurities for fear of losing all.

Many people are surprised at how some 'good matches' end up so bad. There can be many reasons, but God would want us first to check our ability to be intimate. True intimacy requires an opening up of one's life. This in turn requires an unveiling of one's own heart. One cannot have a mature marriage unless he is personally mature. Intimacy can grow only as the couple personally grows.

Transformation to Devotion (Song of Solomon 6:3)

"I am my beloved's and my beloved is mine."

Look carefully and note what the difference is between this line and the former one. Look carefully. It marks the first transformation needed for a married couple to have greater intimacy.

That's right. The two concepts in the sentence have switched places. In the first statement, she sees as most important what she gets out of the marriage. She focuses on having him. It is still true of course, but it no longer her foremost thought. For a while, she focused on what she had through her relationship with him. This has been released. What now is most important?

WHAT'S THE TRANSFORMATION?

"I am my beloved's" has stepped up to first place. She now focuses on her wonderful calling as his wife. The progression is natural and good. The longer she is married and knows more deeply her husband's love, she can deepen her own commitment to God's calling for her. This results in a more faithful form of devotion. Proverbs 31 reminds us of the woman who has been faithful to her calling as wife. She is not focused on what she gets but on what she can give. A sacrificial spirit is critical to a great marriage. It only comes about when we can understand our own calling and motivate ourselves to serve in light of that calling.

Transformation to Surrender (Song of Solomon 7:10)

"I am my beloved's and his desire is for me."

The most intense and mature kind of intimacy and trust is seen in this final phrase. What is the difference between this and the two above? Surrender marks the third transformation.

We first see that the "He is mine" is gone. She no longer focuses on what she got – her man (though she indeed did). Nor should we conclude that she no longer valued him. Although a lessening of value does happen in many marriages, couples in such a circumstance would not speak these words. We must be careful to differentiate between the two. The trust between them has greatly grown so that they can reach this mark of surrender.

She does not change the place of the "I am my beloved's." This is where it should be. What characterizes her life is her devotion to him. She belongs to him. This is the way 'oneness' integrates itself into the practical aspects of marriage. The wife must see herself primarily as his helpmate. She is there for him. As Paul says, "The woman was made for man." But we do see one added change here that marks this crowning intimacy.

She rests herself in her husband's unconditional love. She says, "His desire is for me." This expression has come through many years of regular and constant love. She is not just stating what she hopes is true. This is often said of an immature love. He is there by her side, though, not because of sex and beauty. No. In a great marriage the husband has shown his persis-

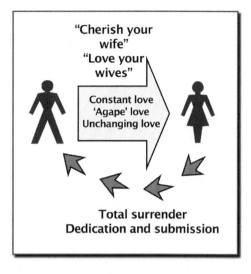

tent faithfulness even in her moody times.

Once this thought dawns on the wife, a greater change comes over her. She becomes totally secure and fulfilled in knowing of his love for her. It is this very love that is alluded to in Ephesians 5:27, "having no spot or wrinkle or any such thing; but that she should be holy and blameless." Love sifts out our sins because it acts as a mirror reflecting them in our faces. Our worries, fears and other sins become great stains on a beautiful tapestry. We desire them to be gone.

The steps to intimacy are gradual but real. She would say that she knew of his love for her all along. He has expressed it ten thousand times in a thousand ways but finally there is a new satisfying and fulfilling awareness that he really does love her. He has devoted himself to her for no other reason than that he likes being with her. This brings her to a new rich and satisfying selfless devotion.

Spiritual

We can see these stages of intimacy in a Christian's life too. Are we surprised? We shouldn't be. The parallel is complete in this sense. God desires us. He really has chosen us for eternity. In a truly humble and grateful spirit we cry out with thankfulness that the Creator of the universe has chosen us, sacrificially given Himself for us and in Christ involved us in God's rich redemptive plan for all eternity. His love invokes unending devotion and joy.

Our Christian lives must go through the commitment and devotion phases, and then right on through to the surrender stage. It is not enough to be baptized and state the catechism. That is religion. God had greater purposes than mere association. Nor does God ultimately want the works – the devotion. That is great. But when we tie all of that together in surrender to the knowledge of His love for us, we cry out "O gracious God, why me!" We cannot fathom His divine love. It is like stepping over the edge of a towering cliff into the vastness of God's eternal love. It overwhelms us with fullness and joy. Truly this is what Paul the apostle has mentioned in his letter,

> *That He would grant you, according to the riches of His glory, to be strengthened with power through His Spirit in the inner man; so that Christ may dwell in your hearts through faith; and that you, being rooted and grounded in love, may be able to comprehend with all the saints what is the breadth and length and height and depth, and to know the love of Christ which surpasses knowledge, that you may be filled up to all the fulness of God (Ephesians 3:16-19).*

Marriage is not just trying to stay out of fights. Marriage is not just tolerating each other's existence. If this is where your marriage is at, then know that God has a long way to take you, but every step is worth it. The good news is that He is with you. He knows full well how to take you there. We all are somewhere on the journey. The main point is that what we have can get better! We do not tolerate inferior marriages because we all can have something so much more splendid, a great marriage and a wonderful relationship with the Lord Himself.

Summary

Intimate marriages are rarely seen. As long as we focus on what we have or want, our old identity (self) shows through. In marriage, we must shed our focus on self. We must put away 'our own' life. Just as the "He is mine" faded away, so we no longer talk about our rights and make demands. Marriage is not about us getting our fair share our rights. One great step toward intimacy comes when there is a loss of focus on self. It is only then that we can focus on what God has called us to do: serve the other.

Intimate marriages are about devotion, joy and focused care on the 'best half.' There is a response mechanism that goes beyond our mere responsibilities – the rules. There is a thrill about serving each other in the capacities in which God has called us. Yes, we are serving our spouses, but there is a deeper commitment to making our spouses greater people. There is the sense of God's calling to better our partner through our acts of devotion.

Great marriages are intimate marriages because there is nothing greater than being caught up in the other's love. The way this love shapes itself will take different forms for a man or a woman. Though both of their hearts are to be shaped by the love and devotion to God, man and woman express their devotion through a different calling within marriage. The man delights in loving his wife unconditionally. The wife takes great joy in the awesome knowledge of his love for her and responds with a deeper devotion. They are different and yet the same. In both cases they focus on their own responsibilities and at the same time find even greater fulfillment through the other's commitment toward themselves.

The world's concept of marriage suffers so greatly because it is so far removed from God's design. They have the promises, but they do not take advantage of them. These two triads in the Song of Solomon alert us to what makes a great marriage. We need a growing relationship with God and each other so that we can step into intimacy with our spouse. Intimacy cannot grow without trust.

Triad #1 speaks of the growing trust that enables us to unfold our hearts before our partners.

Triad #2 clarifies the three transformations that enable a couple to get where God desires to take them.

God has taken this wayward man (me) who did not know how to love and brought him to know the love of God. Through this process the Lord has incredibly blessed our marriage. By meditating on God's perspective of me and my life, I could then begin to think more like God and escape my negative, untrue and destructive spirit. My life became another of Jesus' delightful miracles.

On my own, I would never have been able to provide that constant love that my wife is to be given. My relationship with her would have been poisoned by my critical spirit. Instead, through calculated steps of love, God has led me to ever-deepening trust levels that propel me forward, whether in relationship with God or in marriage, in delight and ecstasy.

Personal struggles interfere with the development or maintenance of trust. For this reason it is best to think of marriage as a triangular relationship: The Lord, the husband and the wife. Only then can trust grow and enable a relationship to enter and maintain its destined intimacy.

Chapter #9 Study Questions

1. How does God regularly work in His people's life through the Song of Solomon?

2. Why do those who are deprived of love and acceptance seek relationships outside of their family?

3. What often happens to those married couples who as children experienced bitterness, criticism and lack of affirmation?

4. Write down the verses for the first triad: the path of love.

5. What does "I am black but lovely" refer to?

6. How can it be interpreted on a physical level (guy-girl relationship)? How about Christ's relationship with His people?

7. What are two differences between the world's approach (I am fair) and the Christian's approach (I am black)?

8. What is significant about the verse Song of Solomon 2:1?

9. What are four things that happen in early romance that need to continue to have a growing trust?

10. Write down the three verses that belong to the second triad of verses: The path toward intimacy.

11. What is the difference between 2:16 and 6:3? What is the significance of this?

12. What is the difference between 6:3 and 7:10? What is the significance of this?

13. After picking one of the application and summary points, write down how God is speaking to you about your own life and marriage.

Building a
Great Marriage

#10 Love Never Fails

God has created each of His children to be a conduit of His love. "Love one another." There is no grander place for this to be seen than in marriage. Wherever God's love comes down and touches a heart, people are changed for the good. We can see this when Jesus mingled with the people when walking through their towns. They were loved by Him and loved Him and in the process were transformed. We will also see the same things happen when a husband or wife deliberately chooses to love his or her spouse despite other inclinations.

A) The Channel of Love

To choose love is to respond to God. When God's love is in our relationships, special things occur. As spouses we need to be committed to bringing God's love to our mates. We need to be strategic. Although husbands are especially commanded by God to love their wives, we will see that both husbands and wives greatly shape the beauty of their marriage by deliberately choosing to love their spouse. Maybe you wonder how you can do this.

As Christians, we need to walk closely with God to obtain that love. Only His love can help us maneuver through difficult relationship problems. Love helps us to have the proper personal motivation (love the unlovely), the needed strength (ability to carry out practical acts of love) and design (help with practical ideas). All through the gospels Jesus  regularly took time to be alone with His Father. This enabled Him to be a vessel that His Heavenly Father used to bring His love and healing to people. In a similar way, we need to meet regularly with God to know how best we can show God's love to our spouse. Let me share a story with you about a practical way to show God's love.

A Love Story

This past week I made a daring adventure, a love adventure. Last year was our 25th wedding anniversary. Unfortunately we couldn't get away for an overnight trip. But we did not simply forget about it either. Several months ago we were talking and wondering whether we could get away for an overnight trip this year – without the children, of course. It sounded good to me. I, as the husband, needed to make three things happen:

(1) I needed to believe that we could get it done with God's help (faith).

(2) I also needed to have the idea or vision for an overnight wedding anniversary trip (hope). I needed one more thing, however.

(3) I actually needed to make loving plans and carry them out (love).

In this case we had several challenges. Many would think our chief concern was finding someone to care for our eight children. However, with two older daughters, this was not a problem for us at this point in life. Though to be honest, it is always a struggle for a mother to leave her little ones. This was true for Linda, too. Our greatest challenge was finding the time. This was one of the busiest times in our lives. I am in the midst of teaching four series and preparing many of those materials for the web.

Guess when our anniversary falls? Right smack in the middle of this extremely busy time. It would have been easy for me to say that we would go later. I believed, however, this was the right time. But something more, I believed that God could help us finish all of our work so that we could spend fifty hours together in some romantic spot. Why? God had been deliberately training us over the previous two months about how He would help us overcome all sorts of obstacles to get His work done. I decided if He could help us then, why not with this situation as well. After all, is it not our Lord who told us to love one another?

Of course, we needed to look at our schedules. Fortunately, one teaching series just ended so we had an open window. Then we saw the right-priced travel deal. The hope for this trip had been there for over a year. The Lord provided us with the faith that enabled us to actually do it. Now, however, I needed to make reservations and start preparing to be away. We actually got away, just the two of us.

All went well on the trip. We just got back and had a wonderful time. God arranged this get-away and enabled us to thoroughly enjoy it. Linda did not need to worry about the children, nor did I need to worry about the work still waiting to be done. Instead we could reflect on our past 26 years together and look ahead to our years to come. The more we celebrate our oneness and in different ways affirm it, the easier it is to put off the difficulties that are associated with a 'two-ness' life.

God's Greater Way

1 John 4 shows us how love has penetrated our world. We need to constantly remind ourselves that the source of love is God Himself. He first loved us.

We love, because He first loved us (1 John 4:19).

As His children, God no longer allows us to say, "I can't love" or "It is too hard." Did you notice that this verse does not only speak of God's love for us through Christ? It also states in clear words that, "We love." On Judgment Day, God will not tolerate all those excuses about busyness, poverty, inability, lack of affection, etc. God changed our whole orientation to this problem when He sent His Son Jesus Christ into the world. By becoming God's children, we are now able to tap into His powerful source of grace to carry out this love.

If you ever begin to sense a loss of interest in loving your spouse, give up hope that your love is effective or simply do not think your love is good enough, refresh yourself in God's presence. There before the Lord you can gain that vision and grace to carry out that love. "We love, because He first loved us." Some people ask, "If we are but a vessel that is pouring out God's love, then we are no longer doing the loving, are we?" Of course we are.

The above verse states that God's love becomes integrated into our lives. How does this happen? When we meet Him each day, we talk to Him and read His Word. We get to know Him more and more. His mindset and devotion become more and more our own. Although we might look for breakthroughs, it is more important that we

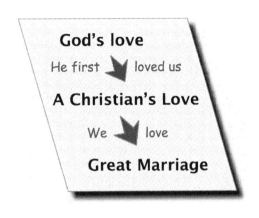

focus on the life commitment of meeting in the Lord's presence, seeking His grace to fill our lives. We are greatly indebted to God for His great love for us (Psalm 116:1). As God's love flows into our own lives, it can flow into our lives and marriages. Only regular intimate contact with God keeps the river of love from running dry.

This is the reason we simply state that one of the most important things needed for an ongoing love of our spouse is to meet personally with God on a regular basis. Do you meet with the Lord every day? How can you reflect His love if you do not regularly meet with Him in a personal way?[64]

Let's draw near to Him now in a prayer:

Dear Father in Heaven, imitation love just isn't going to make it in our world. It is not good enough for our marriages. Cheap human love does not bear, endure and persist. We are impatient, unkind and outright rude. Our so-called love is not love. We need to get deeper Lord. We need to seek Your face for your divine and glorious love to spring forth in our hearts and marriages. If we are content with a cheap love, break us until all the contamination of the

---

[64] If you do not know what personal devotions are or they have become rather stale, study through BFF's "Renewing Your Personal Devotions" series.

world falls off. Reveal the greater glory of the heavenly love. It is time that all of our marriages be touched with Your divine love for You are love.

By this time you are probably wondering what does divine love looks like in a marriage. Fortunately, God has given us a great practical description of this love. 1 Corinthians 13 is the great 'Love' chapter of the Bible. What makes it so? I believe it is because the true character and power of love is revealed. It is much like looking at the sun. We are forced to turn away from it because of the powerful way God's love is revealed to us. Do remember now, that all genuine love is like this. This is what love is. Genuine love can withstand the great pressures that earthly love cannot. Our upbringing is good to a certain point, but it never really endures.

B) The Description of Love (1 Corinthians 13:4-8a)

Although many people would claim to love, only some of them have been seized by its magnificent power, insight and commitment. We see the shallowness of people's commitments when those who take their marriage vows state that they will stay married "as long as we both shall love." Truly, they do not have any notion of what true love is. The true marriage vow states, "As long as we both shall live." Love by definition has many components and without them that professed love simply is not God's kind of love.

Love is patient, love is kind, and is not jealous;
love does not brag and is not arrogant,
does not act unbecomingly; it does not seek its own,
is not provoked, does not take into account a wrong suffered,
does not rejoice in unrighteousness, but rejoices with the truth;
bears all things, believes all things,
hopes all things, endures all things.
Love never fails.

Let us take a look at each of these fourteen components, and what they look like in the context of marriage.[65] This hopefully will give us a better glimpse of how God's love lives itself out in our marriage relationships.

---

[65] Some components are easier to understand than others. We should remember that the original context is a letter that the apostle Paul wrote to a divisive church body. Instead of working toward the welfare of the whole, they focused on their own fleshly thoughts. A couple can also use these verses to gain a picture of true love.

#1 Love is patient

Do I express a forbearing spirit that enables me to listen to and care for my spouse?

Description of Love

The loving spouse does not insist on his own schedule and time constraints. People, especially hurt people, can absorb much time. They often require a lot of time at inconvenient times. The patient spouse trusts God with his very limited time, money, energy, etc. The patient spouse trusts God for wisdom to kindly care for his or her mate.

Situation

- Late again for dinner

- Spoken rudely to

- I don't feel like it (sexual intimacy)

The Path of Love

- "Could we arrange a time to talk about our planning time?"

- "When you say it that way it hurts. Could you make that suggestion in this way, ...?"

- "Oh, what is wrong? If you would like, we can wait."

- "Why are you making me late again!"

Rejection of Love

- "Yea, is that so. We'll you are not so perfect yourself."

- "Well aren't you being selfish!"

#2 Love is not jealous

Do I get jealous or envious at the attention my spouse gets?

Description of Love

Jealousy and envy are the same word in Greek. By pursuing after what one's mate has, it reveals a basic discontent with one's own friends, situation or person. The focus on what one does not have brings him or her to think in opposition to his spouse. Love commits itself to bringing benefit to the other person.

Situation

- Attention received

- Friends

- Fringe benefits

- Health advantages

The Path of Love

- "That was nice you could say that to him."

- "I'm so happy for him!"

- "I focus on excelling on what responsibilities God has given to me."

Rejection of Love

- "Why did you say that to her?" (Suspicious)

- "Why does he get all the attention?"

- "It's easy for him. I just watch these kids all day long." (self-pity)

#3 Love does not brag

Do I tell about my great accomplishments in such a way that makes my spouse feel 'small'?

Description of Love

This person holds back from impressing his spouse. In order to brag or boast, a spouse often is willing to say how much better he is than his spouse and thus state the inferiority of his spouse. Love enables a spouse to see the great things in his spouse and speak of these things.

Situation

- Degrees

- Awards

- Positions

- Money

- Publicity

The Path of Love

- "Are you having trouble with that? Would you want me to help you?"

- Be quiet about how certain God-given gifts have enabled you in certain ways.

Rejection of Love

- "Did you hear how I ...?"

- "Why can't you ...?" (Make the other feel stupid).

- "Oh, I've never had that problem. Why can't you ...?"

#4 Love is not arrogant

Do I think my needs are more important than my spouse's?

Description of Love

The loving person thinks highly of his spouse. He or she is important to his or her welfare. Because the arrogant person thinks more highly of him (her) self, he treats his spouse poorly, thinking he is to be served. Love prefers the spouse over his/her desires.

Situation

- Cleaning a mess

- Having a servant mind

- Making nice compliments

The Path of Love

- "Can I help you clean that?"

- "Is there anything I can help you with?"

- "I appreciate how you do that. It really helps me so much."

Rejection of Love

- "If I was doing it, I wouldn't ..."

- "I can get by without you!"

- "What did you do that for? That was stupid!"

#5 Love does not seek its own

Do I seek the things that I like more than what my spouse prefers?

Description of Love

A loving spouse seeks the welfare of his or her spouse. If we prefer ourselves, then we will give ourselves preferential treatment. We will even lie, cheat, backbite, slander, etc. to serve our own needs over our spouses.

Situation

- Ignore responsibility so one can please himself.

- Break morals to gain one's own desires.

The Path of Love

You say, "Why don't you take a nap. You don't feel too well. I'll help you clean up around the kitchen." (motive good)

Rejection of Love

You suggest, "Why don't you take a rest." Pretends caring for her when all he really wants is to view an uninterrupted sport's game (motive is selfish).

#6 Love is not provoked

Does your spouse easily upset you during his or her irritable times? Do you feel inferior, humiliated or just 'put down'?

Description of Love

The loving spouse does not easily get upset with his spouse. He loves her/him. He might be inconvenienced or his pride attacked, but true love is not easily shaken. Pretend love quickly changes moods, but genuine love is not provoked.

Situation

- Spouse is angry and yelling.

- Spouse is irritable because it is hot out.

- Your wife's critical monthly moody time.

The Path of Love

- "Could we please talk about this a bit later? Our voices are getting too loud."

- (Don't say anything; just keep enjoying your day.)

- Instead of getting upset, you use that energy to do something extra nice for her.

Rejection of Love

- "My fault you say! Well you have it all wrong!"

- "Why do you always have to ruin a great day with your comments!"

- "If I can't do anything right, then why did we get married!"

#7 Love does not take into account a wrong suffered

Do I quickly forgive my spouse and refuse to get bitter?

Description of Love

The loving spouse does not get bitter. Wounded, hurt and mistreated she might be, but love always forgives. She does not store up memories of wrong or plan for revenge. Love daily wipes clean the account of wrongs which enables her to keep caring for the needs of his spouse.

Situation

- Forgot to do something important

- Said something mean to you

- Refuses sex

The Path of Love

- "I was hurt a lot. Thanks so much for straightening things up. It is so much better!"

- "Please forgive me."

- "I forgive you."

Rejection of Love

- "No. I remember last time you really blew it."

- "Don't bother me!"

- "I hate you."

- "I cannot ever forgive you. Even if I could, I wouldn't."

#8 Love does not rejoice in unrighteousness

Do I take a sense of pleasure when my spouse agrees to do evil?

Description of Love

The loving spouse is sad of any kind of evil found in his spouse. He never encourages wicked behavior and rejects the temporary gains to be won from it.

Situation

- Watching a sensual or violent movie together

- Going gambling together

- Lie about something together

- Switch partners

The Path of Love

- "I really desire to be with you but I cannot watch things that displease the Lord."

- "But we are not everyone. I can't sign that form."

- "God doesn't want us to use that money."

Rejection of Love

- "Why don't you watch this with me?" (Dirty or violent film).

- "Everyone else cheats on their taxes."

- "I knew that bet would pay off!"

#9 Love rejoices with the truth

Do I delight in seeing how God helps our marriage in so may ways through observing His truth?

Description of Love

The loving spouse has a great delight when he sees God working in his spouse's life through his or her obedience to God's Word. Love's companion is truth where the light brightly shines and breaks apart lies and unfaithfulness.

Situation

• Worry

• Fears

• Trusting financially

• Sovereignty

The Path of Love

• "Although we might go without because of that decision, I am glad we did the right thing."

• "Did you notice the great way God has overcome our fears?"

Rejection of Love

• "I can't. I'm too fearful."

• "I am so worried that I can't do what I should be doing."

• "No." (Refuses to apologize.)

#10 Love bears all things

Do I shoulder the burden and pain that comes from my marriage so that we might gain an even better marriage?

Description of Love

The loving spouse is willing to put up with all sorts of pain, insult and even injury so that he might like Christ cover the incident with love. By bearing all things, love can withstand the great shocks of rudeness, sin and absolute depravity. Out from the mucky waters grows the white lily flower.

Situation

- Physical pain

- Emotional pain

- Insult

- Isolation

The Path of Love

- "I will forgive you. I have decided that I need to accept the pain that I have suffered from you just as Jesus did. There is no way to pay that back."

- Rejection of Love

- "The pain is too great. I just can't."

- "Why should I forgive you?"

- "You hurt me. I'll never forgive you."

#11 Love believes all things

Do I trust God for help, strength and renewal for each marital difficulty that I face?

Description of Love

The loving spouse trusts God and His perfect design of marriage. He refuses to react to his spouse but instead trusts God for strength and wisdom to properly care for his or her spouse.

Situation

- An unfaithful spouse

- In sickness

- In extreme busyness

- One spouse gives up on a certain area of their marriage

The Path of Love

- "God has given me special grace to love the one that does not love me."

- "I can't do it in my own strength but God is my help."

- "Someway God will work it out for a greater good."

Rejection of Love

- "I can't trust you anymore."

- "I don't think anything good can come out of this marriage."

- "I want out."

- "Here are the divorce papers."

#12 Love hopes all things

Do I treat each challenge in my marriage with a generous dose of expectation that God can somehow do something special even in the most desperate situations?

Description of Love

The loving spouse has an inner aspiration to make his or her marriage work. He is not blind to the problems. The difference is solely in how God can make each case into a special opportunity to serve and display God's love. God's grace can shine into the darkest places.

Situation

- Critical spouse

- An affair

- Alcoholism

- Pornography

The Path of Love

- "God will somehow work it out."

- "God's way is always greater."

- "We just need to trust in Him."

Rejection of Love

- "How could I ever live with him after that?"

- "I just can't go on."

- "I will never forgive him!"

- "I deserve something better."

#13 Love endures all things

Have I made a commitment to love and prize my spouse? Have I recently renewed that commitment?

Description of Love

The loving spouse has chosen to love for life. The commitment is a one-time affair, but the opportunities are spread over their married life. Our love is limited but when God's love fills us, then nothing can stop it. God's love endures shame, reproach, evil, and humility just as God's love in Christ pursued all these things so that we could receive that love.

Situation

- Time

- Poverty

- Sickness

- Trials

The Path of Love

- "What you said and did hurt me a lot, but I have committed myself to serve you for life. Nothing is going to change this. This is my life. It might be more pleasant or hard, but I am going to love you with God's love."

Rejection of Love

- "I give up."

- "I can't put up with this another minute."

- "I must have married the wrong person."

#14 Love never fails

Am I confident of the power of God's penetrating love in every aspect of my marriage?

There are no limitations with God's divine love. God's love does not stop with the sunset or begin with the new week. Divine love will always continue throughout time and eternity. In the darkest of nights, there will always be the eternal light of God's love. Love will outshine hatred and penetrate the vilest deed though it might need to be through sacrifice. May we love our spouse as He has loved us in Christ.

*Love is patient,
love is kind, and is not jealous;
love does not brag and is not arrogant,
does not act unbecomingly; it does not seek its own,
is not provoked, does not take into account a wrong suffered,
does not rejoice in unrighteousness, but rejoices with the truth;
bears all things, believes all things, hopes all things, endures all things.
Love never fails;*

Love never fails. This capstone upon the description of love is not a simple monument but a clear testimony of the most powerful force on earth. When we choose to give up and choose other than love, we simply are allowing the darkness of the world to seize our marriage. It was like the engine in my car that finally seized up after 150,000 miles. The friction was too much, the lubrication too little. It froze. Without God's love, this will happen to all of our marriages.

God's love, however, can take any devastating and dark situation and shine God's light into it. This is what God did with Jesus Christ. Read darkness cannot be overcome with darkness.

> *The light still shines in the darkness and the darkness has never put it out. (John 1:5 Philips).*

The same is true with God's powerful force of love. Notice how faith and love are joined together.

> *By this we know that we love the children of God, when we love God and observe His commandments. For this is the love of God, that we keep His commandments; and His commandments are not burdensome. For whatever is born of God overcomes the world; and this is the victory that has overcome the world--our faith. And who is the one who overcomes the world, but he who believes that Jesus is the Son of God? (1 John 5:2-5).*

The question is not whether you can have a great marriage. The question is whether you will choose to have one. As God's child you have the key to a great marriage. It is God's divine love.

Many people think that it rests with their own emotional love. This is what happens to new couples. They live in love for a while but that emotion fades, and they no longer have the emotional strength to cover or overlook the sins of their spouse.

Others think it requires the dutiful and wearisome carrying out of his or her marital duties. Whether it is cutting the lawn, washing dishes, or having sex, they plug away. They think this is the ultimate of marriage. God in 1 John 5:2-3 says that keeping His commands are not burdensome. What he means is that when we begin to catch the heart of serving, every wall or door becomes an opportunity. There is no end to finding more grace to serve the other in these opportunities.

As long as we are faithful serving, God's love is alive and flowing through our own lives and into our marriage. In most cases this love will begin to touch your spouse's life, though there is no guarantee that it will happen tomorrow. It is our commitment to love for life that never changes.

The Detour of Love

I started this chapter with an example from our recent anniversary celebration. Allow me to share one more typical scene to show you how love works itself out.

We were already two hours late leaving on our get-away trip. That was all right; we were both busy. We had a four-hour trip ahead of us. I wanted to leave early to miss rush hour traffic and long immigration lines. With this two hour loss, we were sure to hit lots of traffic. This is not what we wanted! About two hours into the trip, we were talking about the rest of our trip. Linda mentioned how she would love to dip her feet in the waters of Lake Erie. All I thought about was long slow-moving lines of cars. You can see the analytical man and the feeling woman in conflict. We were not arguing. The conflict was in my mind.

She would like to do this one thing. I thought it best to push forward just in case we could beat rush hour. But the purpose of the trip was to enjoy each other's company. So I seriously considered her real desire and took the scenic route that went along the coast. This, of course, made our trip longer, but in the end we found that this way actually was better. We both thoroughly enjoyed this unplanned detour. The only thing that made us both enjoy it, however, was that I remembered how God speaks through my wife. I need to value her along with her joys and delights. By taking that detour and regularly paying attention to my wife's insights, our marriage is all the more tremendous and wonderful.

And guess what? Along that road we found a state park that did not charge to use their facilities that day (we had very little money). We went down to the shore and had the whole park to ourselves. We had a nice picture by the lilac bushes in bloom. Linda got to wet her feet in the waters of Lake Erie. We had the most pleasant drive possible on that lake shore road. Instead of fighting traffic we were celebrating our 25 years of marriage together.

The wrestling of wills will always be there, sometimes stronger than at other times. But we need to remember God's greater purpose. By choosing to serve one another, we have made the best choice. When we make the best choice of love, we gain the reward. In this case it took a subjugation of my reasoning in order to be able to prioritize her ideals and good pleasures. For me it was going out of the way. But it really was going the right way of love. Love always takes us onto the path of service.

I should add that regarding the trip and which way we went, she was also loving. She was not demanding. She did not seem like she would be at all resentful if I had chosen not to go that way. She only kindly shared with me some of her thoughts and ideals. She allowed me to work through this situation in my own mind and trusted God for the results. Her kind and winsome words made me really want to please her. In the end I found myself asking her to find a possible route that we could take to the shore. Interestingly, we found that 'detour' so nice that we even took it on the way back home.

Summary

We cannot lose with love, but we can lose without it. Satan sometimes tricks us into thinking that our spouse is the enemy to a good life. This is absolutely not the case. God has proclaimed that we are one. Love is the basic way to work out our good and kind deeds toward our spouse to preserve and deepen our relationship.

From a quick look at this description of God's love, we should recognize that our ability to love is wrapped up in how much we are growing as a Christian. We need to keep growing so that we can regularly commune with God, and He with us. God has designed our marriages to be the place that we can work through some of our personal struggles to grow with God and grow in our marriages.

We all can have 'Great Marriages.' God is at work to give us what we so desperately need. Now if we would just begin to choose to consistently love. Start with one day at a time. Early each day cry out, "God help me to love my spouse today. Give me strength. Give me creativity." Do this for a week. Then commit yourself to God again each week to love your spouse in this way. Keep at it. Then commit to loving your spouse each month. Finally, then, reach that delightful spot of committing yourself to your spouse in this way for your whole life. My life is to be fully devoted to kindly caring for my spouse.

God's solution, "Love never fails" might seem rather idealistic, but He knows that it works. He loved the world and sent His only Son to die on the cross for His people's sins. He knew that love would cost Him dearly but that it would also supply what was needed to accomplish His great plan for His stubborn people whom He had decided to intensely love. Love never fails. God always wins. Love always wins. Today, be strategic. Choose His way of love, and you will build up a great marriage.

Put me like a seal over your heart, like a seal on your arm. For love is as strong as death, jealousy is as severe as Sheol; Its flashes are flashes of fire, The very flame of the LORD.

Many waters cannot quench love, nor will rivers overflow it; If a man were to give all the riches of his house for love, it would be utterly despised." (Song of Songs 8:6-7).

If love did not need to work itself out in a practical sense, then God would have been satisfied with the mere idea to save us. Genuine love not only knows what is best but also devotedly implements it. We should only be satisfied with the best! That is God's good plan.

Love excels by accomplishing what we find most difficult to do:

waiting rather than demanding;

extending tender care to obstinate people;

determining to fulfill the needs of others at cost to one's own needs and desires;

acknowledgment of our weaknesses rather than clamoring for compliments.

Love excels by daily revealing God's glory.

Love is God.

The Beauty of Marriage

God still works
miracles.

God wants to work with
us to build a great
marriage.

Building great
marriages is a process
needing time.

It takes time because
we need to be
changed.

Chapter #10 Study Questions

1. How do we bring God's love into our marriages?

2. How do we increase our knowledge of God's love?

3. What were the three things needed for that man to get out on an overnight anniversary trip?

4. How did God train the husband so that he had faith to trust God regarding his work?

5. Can we make any excuses for not loving? Why not (see 1 John 4:19)?

6. Write down and memorize 1 Corinthians 13:4-8a together with your spouse.

7. Which three statements of 1 Corinthians 13 challenge you the most in your marriage? Why?

8. "Love _____ fails" is the key phrase for this chapter. Do you really think that God's love can help every marriage? Why or why not?

9. Are you conscious of how one must go out of his or her way to serve one's spouse?

10. How does one's Christian growth affect the welfare of a person's marriage?

Our Wish for You!

A great marriage requires deliberate and purposeful action through a host of small kindly deeds, gestures and words. Nothing is immediate. The opportunities to build up your marriage are usually found in small unnoticed deeds. Your spouse might not notice. Most important, however, is your own deep, underlying commitment. It will be observed and much appreciated.

A great marriage is what we wish for you. Never be content with only a good marriage. A good marriage is tolerable but has inherent flaws which may become bigger problems later. Why not give up that extra layer of self and push for an even greater marriage? Only in a great marriage is God's glory fully revealed. It is here that His love is being worked out in that 'oneness' relationship.

We are not saying that we have a perfect marriage. The word 'perfect' is inappropriate because we are still sinners. But we can have a great marriage even in our sinful, fallen world because a great marriage does not depend on a perfect life (which we do not have) or a perfect partner (which we do not have) but on forbearance, patience, trust and love. Love triumphs in difficult circumstances.

Treasure your spouse. Set your heart on loving your spouse in whatever circumstance you find yourself. Kind deed by kind deed, smile by smile, grace by grace, you will, by the grace of God, establish a great marriage that will reflect God's glorious love and person.

Appendix 1: More on the Authors

We (Paul & Linda) both grew up in the same city north of Boston, MA in the United States but only got to know each other after high school. We have been married 35+ wonderful years and have been raising our children for all but one year!

Challenging years, financial hard times, eight children (now three grandchildren) and busy ministry life did not allow for much romance. God's biblical principles when practically understood, however, have enormously helped us in our marriage.

Rev. Paul Bucknell, president and founder of *Biblical Foundations for Freedom*, travels internationally giving workshops on marriage, parenting and other topics to pastors and Christian leaders. He has written sixty articles on marriage alone and more then ten books on many different aspects of Christian life.

(More on Paul, Linda and the ministry)[66]

---

[66] http://www.foundationsforfreedom.net/Help/AboutBFF/Biography.html

Made in the USA
Columbia, SC
27 September 2023

23405608R00165